INDIVIDUALIZED
READING INSTRUCTION

Roland West

INDIVIDUALIZED READING INSTRUCTION

Its Implications for the Teacher and Librarian

Published for the Graduate Faculty,
C. W. Post College of Long Island University
by
KENNIKAT PRESS
Port Washington, N. Y.

INDIVIDUALIZED READING INSTRUCTION

Published for the Graduate Faculty,
C. W. Post College of Long Island University by
Kennikat Press
Library of Congress Catalog Card No: 64-15548
ISBN 0-8046-0496-7

Manufactured by Taylor Publishing Company   Dallas, Texas

CONTENTS

ACKNOWLEDGMENTS

THE AUTHOR is deeply grateful for the encouragement and stimulus given by his colleagues and his mentors at the C. W. Post School of Library Science. The author thanks the many authors and publishers for their kind permission to quote extensively from the many sources cited in the text.

Particular mention must be made of the constant advice and counsel offered by three outstanding librarians and teachers—Miss Christine Gilbert, Mr. John Gillespie and Mr. Paul Riley. Finally, to Professor E. Hugh Behymer, Director of the School of Library Science at C. W. Post College of Long Island University the author extends his special thanks and appreciation.

R. W.

INDIVIDUALIZED
READING INSTRUCTION

I. BACKGROUND AND DESCRIPTION OF THE STUDY

BACKGROUND OF THE STUDY

Most thoughtful people today are well aware of the importance of knowing how to read with efficiency and understanding. Since 1524, when Martin Luther initiated education for the common man so that each might read the Bible for himself, various methods of teaching people how to read have appeared. Reading was stressed in early America, first for the same religious reasons that motivated Luther, and later, when freedom was won from England, because it was generally realized that there is a relationship between the ability to read intelligently and the ability to vote intelligently. As the nation has moved forward from those comparatively simple times, the importance of knowing how to read and to read effectively has grown more acute. Reasons for developing individual reading power range from the use of reading to simply get along from day to day—take the right bus, find the right telephone number, or select the right product wisely—to the more complex uses of reading to earn a living, expand and deepen educational experiences, and escape from the tensions of modern competitive society.

Methods of teaching young people to read have developed historically from the alphabet and spelling systems to the word, sentence, and story methods. Attempts have been made by many reading authorities to identify the characteristics of the good reader. Good readers, they usually say, are those who are able to group words into thoughts, read rapidly without loss of comprehension, choose their reading to fit their immediate and long-range needs, and apply what they read; in short, good readers are those who make time in their lives for reading and use reading to influence their lives. Attempts have likewise been made to define effective reading, perhaps none more meaningful and amusing than Mortimer Adler's:

If we consider men and women generally, and apart from their professions and occupations, there is only one situation I can think of in which they almost pull themselves up by their bootstraps, making an effort to read better than they usually do. When they are in love and are reading a love letter, they read for all they are worth. They read every word three ways; they read between the lines and in the margins: they read the whole in terms of the parts, and each part in terms of the whole; they grow sensitive to ambiguity; to insinuation and implication: they perceive the color of words, the odor of phrases, and the weight of sentences. They may even take punctuation into account. Then, if never before, or after, they read.[1]

The alphabet method was the first approach to teaching children how to read which was used in this country. The typical procedure was for the child to first memorize the names of the letters and to identify both the capital and small forms. Spelling and pronouncing combinations of two letters followed, then three-letter combinations, and finally monosyllabic words. Multisyllabic words, phrases, sentences, and stories were gradually introduced. Memorization of prayers, the Ten Commandments, and biblical material was required, and oral reading was stressed. Noah Webster's *American Spelling Book*, popularly known as the "blue-back speller", appeared in the last quarter of the eighteenth century. This widely used textbook for both reading and spelling instruction opened with the alphabet and progressed to letter combinations, stressing pronunciation, enunciation, and articulation, and to interrelated reading and spelling. Reading instruction under the Webster system required that the child laboriously spell out each word that he would need to use in reading sentences and stories included in the book.

The first commercial success in producing a graded series of readers was *McGuffey Readers*, prepared by William Holmes McGuffey. These highly successful readers—it is estimated that between 1836 and 1920 more than 122 million copies were sold—played a significant role in determining many of the dominant attitudes of the American people and were, according to some authors, instrumental in shaping American literary tastes. Mark Sullivan remarked that,

> to nine out of ten average Americans what taste of literature they got from *McGuffey's* was all they ever had; what literature the children brought into the home in *McGuffey's Readers* was all that ever came . . . . McGuffey, in short, because of the leverage of his readers, had a large part in forming the mind of America.[2]

Meanwhile, during the last half of the nineteenth century, the alphabet-spelling method of teaching children to read was gradually replaced by the word method of instruction. As this method gained in general acceptance by educators, parents became disturbed to find that their children often did not know the names of letters in words they could pronounce and that they were sometimes unable to attack new words in unfamiliar settings. In order to remedy this situation, the phonic method was developed in the last quarter of the nineteenth century.[3] Subsequently, modifications of the phonic approach, called phonetic systems, were developed which attempted to provide a symbol for each of the sounds in the English language. However, it was soon found that the effort required in deciphering the phonetic symbols meant a loss of understanding of the meanings of words and that, moreover, children often misspelled words because of false impressions gained from the phonetic systems.

The twentieth century saw a return to the word method, which was expanded to include phrase, sentence, and story approaches to reading and which emphasized thought-getting rather than word-attack mastery. After the First World War, rapid silent reading was stressed as a major objective of the reading program. Objective tests to measure reading achievement were developed, and practice exercises were widely used. The so-called story method of teaching reading gained steadily in popularity after the end of the First World War. This method involved the reading or telling of a story to children by the teacher as they followed along in their books; then they in turn retold or dramatized the story, drilled on words and phrases, and finally read the story themselves. This method, which emphasized drill on whole phrases and sentences as well as on whole words, recognized phonetics as a subsidiary factor only. The content of the story method readers usually consisted of Mother Goose tales, rhymes, fables, and folk tales. This method made its greatest contribution to the reading curriculum in its emphasis on meaningful reading, but it was hampered by the large number of new words that children were required to learn at early levels of instruction.

Mostly because of a strong reaction to the phonetic method of teaching reading, the story method became the predominant instructional technique in the 1920's. According to William Gray, by the late decade teachers were commonly warned by their superiors against giving any special attention to the visual forms of words; meaning was considered to be the only factor in word perception, and children were expected to identify new words largely from the use of context clues.[4] In an effort to overcome the chief disadvantage of the method—the great number of new words introduced in the early readers—the concept of vocabulary control was introduced in the early 1930's. The effort to keep word count low while maintaining interesting content was a difficult one, and the interest factor in the readers' content often suffered as a result.

This concept of controlled vocabulary resulted in the development of several series of basic reading textbooks, the revised editions of which are currently in use in the great majority of elementary school classrooms today. A series of books, in theory, carries the child from the preprimer level of instruction through the sixth or eighth grade reader with careful attention to the number of new words that he encounters in each selection. While all children began with the preprimer in the first grade, it soon became apparent that some children could not proceed from book to book as rapidly as others. During the

1940's, a concerted effort was made by many educators and school supervisers to encourage teachers to divide their classes into subgroups to accommodate varying levels of ability in reading. By the end of that decade the basal reading program with its attendant ability grouping within the classroom was firmly established in most of the elementary schools of the nation.

In effect, the term "basal reading program" implies the use of a series of basic reading textbooks which typically consists of anthologies of largely fictional selections, sequentially and systematically arranged on the basis of the vocabulary control and on the entry that each selection offers into the teaching of the various developmental reading skills. The use of such readers as the foundation of the total reading program in elementary schools usually involves the establishment of relatively homogeneous ability groups within the heterogeneous classrooms. The standard number of reading groups in the typical classroom is three, probably because teachers are unable to efficiently handle a larger number. The criteria for deciding who should be in what group under such a teaching program are usually the scores received by the children in the class on the most recently administered reading achievement test. The most common pattern of organization is for the teacher to group his class into high, average, and low sections and to then furnish each of the groups with a set of basic readers appropriate in difficulty to the central tendency of reading achievement for the group. Then the groups and the teacher proceed to "work through" these texts, taking each story and its related vocabulary, skills, and workbook pages sequentially. Important to the success of the basal reading program is the unity or oneness that must characterize the daily progression of each of the reading groups; there is usually little room in such a program, in practice, for gearing its direction and progress to the interests, pace, and unique needs of each individual member of the group.

About 1950, a reaction to this type of instructional program began to set in.[5] Starting then, and increasing in frequency with the succeeding years, articles appeared in educational journals sharply critical of what was termed the "lock-step" approach taken to reading instruction in basal reading programs. There were several factors that lent impetus to interest in individualized reading as an alternative method of instruction. Certainly a major influence was a dissatisfaction with some of the outcomes of basal reading instruction; some educators began to express a belief that an unjustifiably high incidence of poor or retarded readers was to be found in the public schools of the nation. Then too, several writers pointed out that a growing number of young people had failed to develop any permanent interest in reading as a leisure-time activity. Surveys indicated that large numbers of elementary school children did little reading on their own, that high school students held reading in relatively low esteem, and few adults were found to be widely read. Commenting on the results of these studies, Allan McMahan wrote: "It is estimated that fewer than half the people in the United States ever read a book; fewer than one-fifth of them ever buy a book."[6]

Paul Witty has summarized several other arguments that were advanced by proponents of individualized reading.[7] They asserted that the individualized method of teaching reading could do what the ability-grouped basal reading program could never do—provide for the wide range of individual differences, not only in reading ability but also, and perhaps more importantly, in interests and needs. Critics of the basal reading program emphasized the failure of the basic textbooks to recognize the factor of the child's interest and to utilize the wealth of children's literature. They argued that children's literature should not simply be used as an adjunct or supplement to the reading program but rather as its central core.

By 1952, a more or less clearly defined alternative to ability-grouped basal reading instruction began to emerge in educational literature. Most of the proponents of the plan expressed dissatisfaction with the "lock-step" inefficiency of the basal reading program, its neglect of individual differences, tastes, and abilities, and its failure to stimulate on-going reading interests. There also began to appear a forceful and appealing argument that ability grouping within the classroom for reading instruction is basically an undemocratic practice in that it encourages the creation of a social caste system and a form of social stratification.

Basic to the philosophy of the individualized reading program is the abandonment of basic reading textbooks as the foundation of the reading program and the substitution of a wide variety of both text and trade books. According to the plan, each child, motivated by his own unique interests and needs, selects his own books and reads them under the teacher's guidance, hopefully, during his own free time. The reading periods are usually so organized that the teacher is able to have regular short conferences with each individual student about the book that he is currently reading and the reading problems that he may be encountering. An important part of the program involves a sharing period when children have an opportunity to tell their peers about the content of and their reactions to their books in progress. In most of the reported versions of the program in action provision is made for small group instruction when the teacher's records indicate that a small core of children share some common instructional need, but the structure or membership of such groups is kept fluid and their duration is short-lived.

Educators' interest in and teachers' practice of individualized reading increased rapidly during the past decade. Jeannette Veatch is in agreement with other writers when she states that the individualized method of teaching reading gained national attention—largely through the publication of articles and reports in professional periodicals—in 1952.[8] Perhaps no other methodological movement in educational history has elicited so many contributions from the ranks of practicing elementary school teachers. While some of the educational literature lacks scientific objectivity it is often extremely convincing. Convincing too are the alarmed objections raised by the critics of the movement who express fear that too great a commitment to the philosophy and methodology of individualized reading will lead to a haphazard instructional program in reading. They express concern over what they claim has been the abandonment of sequential skills development in reading instruction and a disregard for strict vocabulary control. Some of the most forceful objections come from nationally recognized experts in the field of reading instruction, many of whom are editors or consultants of basic reading series. Constance McCullough, an editor of the widely used Ginn reading series, has written a typical disparagement:

Much of the knowledge we now have about the teaching of reading has been developed by a curious—and in terms of the lives of the children—wasteful pattern of extremes. We learned a great deal about oral reading by having too much of it, about silent reading by neglecting oral, about extensive reading by neglecting phonics, and speed by neglecting comprehension. We are now involved in a great controversy over the relative virtues of a developmental program with incidental instruction ... Measurement of the success of individualized reading experiments has been limited to cheerful miens, numbers of books read, and scores on survey tests of reading. (In one study, the two groups had not even had the same test.) Obviously, a child free to do as he likes wears a more cheerful face, and if he reads books extensively, he reads more books than a child who spends a considerable time reading intensively with the teacher.[9]

But the equally respected authority on childhood education, Leland Jacobs of Columbia University writes in defense of the program:

As knowledge about learning theory, about child growth and development, about linguistics and communication arts, about the reading act itself has increased, the methods, procedures, and practices through which children are led to fathom the mysteries of the "little black marks" have changed or been refined. In the interest of the child and the culture ... applications of what is salient and pertinent knowledge from such fields as psychology, child study, sociology, philosophy, and linguis-

tics must be translated into educational theory and practice....
The individualizing of reading finds its bearings and garners
its support from research findings that its proponents believe
to be foundational in helping children in reading skills and
abilities . . . . Individualizing reading practices is an attempt on
the part of the teacher so to manage the classroom that each
child is learning to read at his own "growing edges". Respect for
the unique individuality of the child is safeguarded. The child's
purposes and plans are thus intimately involved in establishing the thresholds of his own learnings. Instruction is paced
to the individual's needs, concerns, lacks, aspirations. The selection of reading materials, experiences, and resources is a matter of a particular child's recognition that "This is what I really
want to try to read." The individualizing of reading practices
has already attracted a large number of prospective, creative
teachers who are seeking ways of making the reading act more
pointedly meaningful for every child they teach.[10]

THE NEED FOR A STUDY

Despite some strong resistance from influential quarters, an examination of the professional
and educational literature seems to indicate a
growing acceptance of the philosophy and methodology of individualized reading by educators,
administrators, supervisors and teachers at the
elementary school levels of instruction. Such a
movement has important implications for the elementary school library and librarians; some of
these would seem to be rather obvious, but some
are not so clearly understood.

The 1960 *Standards for School Library
Programs* asserts that the reading ability of the
pupil and his reading interests are a joint responsibility of teachers, librarians, and parents:

The individualized reading program, starting in kindergarten and continuing through each successive grade level, stimulates and motivates the development of good reading habits. The program rests upon and makes extensive use of a rich and varied school library collection that meets the interests and abilities of every student.[11]

The *Standards* goes on to stress the importance of teacher-librarian teamwork in an effective reading program, the importance of the librarian working with all of the teachers responsible for the developmental, corrective, and individualized reading programs in the school. It points out that reading guidance can be more meaningful when the librarian has access to and makes use of reading scores, intelligence quotients, and other pertinent data about the characteristics of individual students. The *Standards* consequently seems to imply that the librarian should be more aware of the processes involved in teaching children how to read than has formerly been assumed necessary. The *Standards* strongly emphasizes the fact that, in the ideal, the librarian should be a key member of the instructional team in reading.

Jean Lowrie has pointed out that, while individualized reading has been an important aspect of the elementary school library program for years,

The trend toward individualized teaching of reading in the elementary school involves a new use of library books and new techniques of library service by librarians . . . . It is necessary that the librarian and the teacher work closely together in guiding the individual reading choices, choosing books to be used in the classroom, and providing supplementary materials. It is necessary that the librarian be conscious of each child's reading ability.[12]

Recently Mary Gaver, professor in the Graduate School of Library Service, Rutgers University, has cited the need for a study of the implications of the individualized reading program for school librarians:

Case studies, experiments, and even status studies or bibliographic surveys are needed to clarify the roles of the elementary school librarian and the library in work with exceptional children and in special teaching situations. . . . The individualized method of teaching reading is much discussed but its implications for libraries are little understood.[13]

DESIGN OF THE STUDY

The investigator has set out to determine, through a study of the philosophy underlying the individualized method of teaching reading and reports of the program in action, what implications this method of reading instruction has for the elementary school librarian. The solution of the problem rests upon finding answers to two basic questions:

1. What are the characteristic aspects of the philosophy and methodology of individualized reading?

2. How can the elementary school librarian help to implement the individualized reading

program and assist in achieving the goals of the program?

In an attempt to find answers to these questions, data will be drawn from the following sources:

1. Articles about individualized reading appearing in educational and library periodicals.

2. Books about the teaching of reading in general and about individualized reading specifically.

3. The investigator's personal experiences over the past five years as a teacher using individualized reading as a method of instruction in his work with fourth, fifth, and sixth graders.

Data gathered from these sources will be categorized for analysis according to the following scheme:

1. Information dealing with the materials of instruction.

2. Information dealing with the organization of the classroom.

3. Information dealing with reading conferences and records.

4. Information dealing with related instructional and creative activities.

5. Information dealing with the evaluation of children's growth in reading.

The intent of the study is not to develop an exhaustive history of the individualized reading movement, but rather to survey the philosophical and methodological aspects of the movement in an attempt to discover useful clues to a definition of the librarian's role in the program. It is felt that such clues will be found in fact or by implication in an examination of the writings of theorists who gave definition and impetus to the movement and the practitioners who reported on their experiences in using the program in the classroom.

The present study has reference to the individualized method of teaching reading only as it specifically relates to the middle grades—fourth, fifth and sixth grade levels—of the elementary school and thus has implications to the elementary school librarian's work with these levels of instruction.

The source literature treated will be limited chronologically to material appearing between January, 1950, and December, 1962.

Basic to the study is the assumption that the individualized method of teaching reading is a movement of genuine significance in modern education and is a part of a larger and more inclusive trend to individualize instructional methods at all educational levels.

Finally, the study involves two basic hypotheses related to the investigation of the movement to individualize the teaching of reading in a search for its implications to elementary-school librarians:

1. A basic requirement for the successful implementation of the individualized method of teaching reading in the elementary school is the expert assistance of a professionally trained librarian working cooperatively with students and teachers.

2. In order to make his most effective contribution to the success of the individualized reading program, the elementary-school librarian needs to be knowledgeable about the methodology involved in teaching children how to read and in promoting their maximum growth in reading power.

II. FORCES LEADING TO INDIVIDUALIZED READING

DISSATISFACTION WITH CURRENT PRACTICES

During the first quarter of the twentieth century there was considerable interest among educators concerning various proposals to individualize instruction in the schools. Russell Stauffer has cited the work of Fredrick Burk, who, convinced that individual differences could not be met under existing patterns of instruction recommended a program of complete individualization and demonstrated some of its values in experimental schools in San Francisco and Los Angeles during the first two decades of the century.[14] Later Carleton Washburn developed a similar technique of instructional organization for the public schools of Winnetka, Illinois. Under the Winnetka Plan each child could take as much time as he needed to master a skill, but he had to master it; thus, time was varied rather than quality. During the same period the Dalton Plan was developed in New York City. This scheme made adjustments for individual abilities, interests, and needs.

The rising birth rate of the period immediately following the First World War and the

growing influence of John Dewey's emphasis on
the importance of shared social learnings in the
classroom were, in part, responsible for a general
loss of interest in individualized methods of instruction. In many schools previously committed
to an individualized approach, there was a tendency to shift emphasis to social activities and
shared learnings. Paul Witty has noted that,
following a rather general acceptance on the part
of educators of the significance of social experiences and shared goals, interest in and the movement towards the individualization of instruction were generally abandoned during the period
from 1925 to 1950.[15]

Some of the major forces leading to a re-
surgence of interest in individualization in reading instruction at the elementary-school level
have already been cited. The late William Gray,
then dean of American reading authorities, summarized these forces as he saw them:

The arguments advanced by its proponents run about as follows: Children differ so widely in interests, capacity to learn,
and motives that it is impossible to provide adequate stimu-
lation and guidance through the use of the same materials and
group instruction. If the child is to develop individuality, creativity, and ability to think clearly and interpret deeply, he
must not be hampered by group regimentation. Instead, he
should learn to read in an environment which stimulates motives for reading, which permits free choice of materials to be
read at his own rate, and receive help as needed, or at scheduled
times.[16]

One of the most comprehensive statements of the dissatisfaction that disturbed teachers and stimulated their interest in an alternative method of teaching reading is furnished by Helen Darrow and Virgil Howes, who worked with a group of over fifty teachers in San Diego, California. Each of the teachers involved in the project had at least five years of experience in teaching. Though their grades and schools differed—some taught in new buildings with the latest facilities, others in older buildings with seats still fastened to runners and lined in straight rows—and the children in their classes ranged in abilities from the highly intelligent to the very limited, from the highly emotional to the optimally well-adjusted, the teachers shared one thing in common: a strongly expressed discontent with the way their reading program was progressing. The kind of reading program that disturbed them, as described by the writers, was the typical ability-grouped basal reading scheme: the children in each class were assigned to one of three ability groups—high, middle, and low—at the beginning of each school year on the basis of reading test scores, and each group was assigned an appropriate set of basic readers. As the school year progressed and the groups worked through their basic readers, something seemed lacking; the teachers experienced an absence of spark, challenge, and satisfaction.

The teachers complained that under the ability-grouped basal reading plan the reading abilities among the children varied so much that it became unrealistic to confine instruction to three groups. The expanse of reading range found in each classroom would necessitate the creation of six or seven reading groups, but working with so many reading groups in the manner of teaching-by-the-manual would consume so much of the class time that other areas of the curriculum would have to be curtailed or possibly abandoned.. While teaching children to read was conceded to be a prime objective of elementary education, a balanced program of learnings and experiences was essential; the problem, then, was how to handle the range of reading abilities within a reasonable amount of time.

Teachers also expressed concern over the fact that too often children waited for the teacher to move them toward reading; that is, they waited until the teacher had started them off and then read only the required material in their basic readers. The teachers wanted the children to read on their own, but, in order to achieve this, the children obviously needed experiences in selecting reading to meet their personal interests and needs. They reasoned that after all, if the purpose of building reading power is to use it in voluntary situations, then the purpose of the program was not being achieved. The teachers found that, in working with basic readers, where selections followed one another systematically within each book and from book to book, it was difficult for them to develop within each child standards of selection and experiences in choosing books for personal satisfaction and enjoyment.

Perhaps the most profoundly disturbing problem, one faced by most teachers who divide classes into ability groups, was the tag effect. With the group as the standard of measurement of progress, individual pupils readily tagged themselves or were tagged by others as "poor readers" or "outstanding readers." Children are rarely able to see themselves under this pattern of organization as moving along a continuum of reading progress, and thus many either showed little incentive to improve or else felt driven to beat the group. Either they had a "what's-the-use?" attitude, "I'm-the-worst-reader-in-my-group" attitude, or they wanted desperately to catch up with the group or get into a superior reading group.

The thorny problem of the social stratification that often takes place when ability grouping is established within the classroom for the purpose of instruction has long disturbed many educators who are aware of how such a system violates democratic principles. Alvina Burrows, a professor at New York University's School of Education, was an early and forceful voice protesting the attendant dangers of dividing classes into ability groups for the purpose of reading instruction. In what was possibly the first book to describe and recommend to teachers the individualized method of teaching reading, she wrote:

The question is no longer whether but how to individualize instruction. . . . To date, the teaching of reading has neglected the strong readers in a sometimes misdirected effort to bring the weaker ones up to grade. The able child deserves the challenge of a forthright meeting of minds in his reading program. The weak ones need the encouragement and confidence of being treated with dignity and respect. The stigma often attached to being a slow reader has no place in a scheme of individualized reading, nor does the high powered reader suffer by not receiving a fair share of time and guidance. Each is accorded the right to make choices, to match interests with appropriate reading content, and to pool his findings with those of the class. Each is offered the stimulus of an adult's sincere response to his satisfactions and success in reading.[18]

Jeannette Veatch, who put together the first book for teachers exclusively devoted to individualized reading instruction,[19] has also cited the undemocratic nature of ability grouping within the classroom for the purpose of teaching reading.

Years ago teachers began separating children into groups or classes of low, medium, or high ability. This was the most effective method of teaching known at the time. However, is the democratic ideal of equal opportunity for all to develop their talents fully, best promoted by ability grouping? This writer thinks not. In the teaching of reading, at least, a methodology has been developed which enables teachers to provide full opportunity for each pupil without using ability grouping.

The process of self-selection of reading matter makes arbitrary separation of children into ability groups unnecessary. The democratic ideal of the uniqueness of the individual and of equal opportunity for growth is provided for. Individual interests and purposes can be realized and abilities can be developed as rapidly or as slowly as inherent growth potential makes possible. The practice of individualizing reading . . . meets the critera of the democratic ideal. Furthermore, it provides an efficient method of meeting the wide range of differences which are common in any classroom group.[20]

In developing her arguments against the prevailing use of the ability-grouped basal reading method of instruction, Miss Veatch posed a number of penetrating questions regarding the basic readers and their use as the foundation of the reading program in the elementary school.[21] Among the questions she asked were:

1. Should basic readers be used basically? The author maintains that, while the teachers' manuals that accompany the basic readers talk about provision for individual needs, in actual practice teachers gear instruction to group needs, because that is the way the reading program is structured. Even if one assumed that the ideal would be a combination of basal reading instruction plus day-to-day provision for individual differences and needs, time pressures in the classroom make the realization of the ideal impossible.

2. Do basic readers lack appeal? The author thinks they do and quotes the opinions of other writers that, despite improvements in format,

basic readers fail to appeal to many children because of the pallid content which is selected into
the readers mainly on the theory that vocabulary must be tightly controlled. Research indicates that there has been a trend towards the re-
duction of vocabulary in recent years, with dras-
tic cuts having been made in the number of new
words introduced in successive books in basic
reader series.[22] There is also the belief by many
of the editors of these readers that new words
must be frequently repeated; thus, at the early
level of instruction there are such sentences as,
"Down, down, came the rain, down, down,
down." If children must be artificially motivated
to read such material, their desire to read will,
consequently, often be reduced.

3. Are basic readers true to life? An analysis
of the content and illustrations of these readers
from the socio-economic class viewpoint, writes
Miss Veatch, indicates that the books invariably
portray an upper middle-class society which is
far removed from life as most children know it.

4. Do basic reader systems subordinate the
real needs of teacher and student to unrealistic
assumption about the teaching-learning process?
The author points out that, while manuals and
workbooks that accompany the basic readers are
designed to supplement the readers and the teaching practices that guide their use, they have at

least two serious flaws: they assume that all children at a given level have similar reading abilities and weaknesses, and they further assume, by the very reason that they call the readers basic that it is possible to devise teaching material that anyone and everyone can use to profit in a given teaching situation. Since comments by supervisors indicate that even the modicum of flexibility that manuals suggest is often ignored by teachers using basic reader series, Miss Veatch advances the hypothesis that the page-by-page nature of the basal reading program discourages teachers from planning their own teaching and, consequently, discourages teacher creativity.

OLSON'S THEORETICAL CONTRIBUTIONS

Such discontent with ability-grouped basal reading instruction as has been described gave rise to interest in an alternative individualized method of instruction. William Sheldon has stated that the advocates of individualized reading took their cue from the studies of Willard Olson.[23] All available evidence supports this contention.

Dr. Olson, as a result of his extensive studies of the nature of child development, evolved a theory of learning that involves three basic concepts: seeking, self-selection, and pacing. This theory was first published in Dr. Olson's text on

child development in 1949. In 1952, the implications of his theory to the reading program in
the elementary school appeared in pamphlet
form, placing the embryonic thinking of the in-
dividualized-reading people on sound psychological and physiological grounds.[24]

Beginning with the observation that the
healthy child is naturally active and exploratory
during his waking hours and that he seeks from
his environment those experiences that are consistent with his maturity and needs, Dr. Olson
noted that other aspects of the environment not
sought out by the child contributed appreciably
little or nothing to the child's learning. Dr.Olson
stated that children develop at such widely varying rates that it is impossible to say when they,
as a group, will be ready for a particular experience but that observation of the seeking behavior of an individual child offers appropriate
clues about his readiness for a learning experience.

This is evident even in the first year of life as the child begins to
understand, later as he begins to talk, and in his early respon-
siveness to pictured materials found in the home. The longer
the children have an opportunity to grow and the more experiences that they have, the more different do they become
and the less ready are they for a common experience—either in
terms of difficulty level or in terms of interest.[25]

Having developed his concepts of seeking and
self-selection, Dr. Olson proceeded to illustrate

how teachers may use them to advance children's competence in school. The artistic and scientific teacher, according to Dr. Olson, is the one who is a close observer of the seeking and self-selective behavior of each individual with whom he works. When a teacher has a high regard for the child's behavior in these respects, the child "grows into the reading experience." Naturally, there are differences in the speed at which this happens; with the accelerated child, it happens so rapidly one is barely able to identify the elements of the method, but the fact is that some children in the third grade are as immature as some in the kindergarten.   If these differences are not taken into account in the classroom, the learning process becomes frustrating and painful for all involved.

Dr. Olson's concept of pacing refers to the acts by the teacher which ensure that each child is provided with the materials that he needs at the time he needs them. Most teachers are aware of the fact that errors in pacing can easily result in a loss of interest in the learner. Holding down the pace when the student is ready for more challenging material leads to boredom and apathy, while speeding up the pace beyond the student's readiness to grasp the material can lead to frustration and hostility. The pacing concept is supported by elements of success, incentive, and

productivity, commonly recognized as crucial
in the psychology of learning.

Studies of learning and productivity in relationship to the goals
that are set suggest that the child will continue to strive when
success is clearly within his grasp. He will start avoiding the
experiences which are at a level of difficulty clearly beyond his
present attainments. The teacher's task is to guarantee that
every classroom situation, or its immediate surroundings, will
have in it tasks which are interesting in terms of the intrinsic
content, and which also cover a range of difficulty as great as
the variability in the human material with which he deals.[26]

Thus did Willard Olson establish the foundation upon which a group of educators, already
deeply disturbed about the nature and practice
of ability-grouped basal reading instruction,
could develop a program in which individual
differences would not only be accepted as a fact
of school life but also be utilized as an integral
factor of another way of reading instruction. His
studies of the nature of growth, behavior, and
achievement in children contributed the concepts of seeking, self-selection, and pacing to
these educators who were reviewing previous
research into the individualization of instruction
for its implications to the development of an alternative reading program.

A NEW PLAN EMERGES

Some of the earliest published writers to encourage teachers to try individualized method of
teaching reading include Alvina Burrows of New

York University, Gertrude Hildreth of Brooklyn
College, Jeannette Veatch of Pennsylvania State
University, and May Lazar of New York City's
Bureau of Educational Research. At the 1957
Conference of the International Reading Association, Dr. Lazar gave a speech in which she described in some detail how the New York City
schools became interested in individualized
reading:

> Too close adherence to grade level standards and the use of
> graded textbooks, which assumed that all children move at the
> same pace, prevented our practices from being as forward-looking
> as our ideas. We began to question the slavish adherence to the
> basic reader systems. There was a strong belief that the mate-
> rials would do the teaching rather than the teacher. There was
> too much confusion between the methods and materials; be-
> tween methods and class organization. There was also too much
> thinking in terms of mechanics rather than in terms of objec-
> tives and values.
>
> We began therefore to sharpen our thoughts in view of our
> findings and to take a new look at the whole program—the
> place of reading in the total curriculum, the materials and meth-
> ods used, and the results in terms of larger values rather than in
> terms of skills alone. In short, were the practices and ap-
> proaches meeting specifically the needs and interests of the
> children? What type of program would really touch the chil-
> dren and make them want to read and love to read?[27]

Dr. Lazar went on to tell how the discontent
with ability-grouped basal reading instruction
and the prevailing beliefs of workers in the Bureau of Educational Research that reading is
"a way of life and not a skills gadget-collecting
procedure" and "that experiences and relation-

ships are closely related to reading activities and that reading is a vital part of the child's full life" caused them to take note of the thinkings and writings of others who were working along the same lines and had published articles about their philosophy in the early 1950's in such professional journals as *Elementary English,Childhood Education,* and the *Reading Teacher.*

Willard C. Olson's studies concerned with the nature of growth, behavior, and achievement led to the concepts of seeking, self-selection, and pacing. Dr. Olson ties up these concepts admirably with the reading program. These studies gave reassurances to our own theories of Individualized Reading. Jeannette Veatch reinforces this with her definition of Individualized Reading: "An individualized reading program provides each child with an environment which allows him to seek that which stimulates him, choose that which helps him develop most, and work at his own rate regardless of what else is going on. . . ."[28]

Most proponents of individualized reading agree that there is no single approach or method of individualized reading. They commonly express the belief that individualized reading is rather a way of thinking about reading instruction, an attitude of the teacher regarding the place of reading in the total curriculum of the elementary school. It involves concepts of classroom organization and ways of working with the materials of education. Jeannette Veatch has stated that individualized reading is characterized by the following features:

It is a method devised to meet individual differences.

Its major feature is that children themselves select their own reading materials.

It allows children to read at their own rate.

It permits teachers to work almost entirely with individuals.

It combines the best elements of recreational reading and one-to-one skill teaching.

It does away with groups based upon ability. When groups are organized, they are only temporary, with a single specific purpose.[29]

When articles first appeared in educational journals describing the individualized method of reading instruction, the system was confused in the minds of some with recreational reading, long a supplement to the basal reading program in some schools. There are, however, very basic and important differences between the two, as Miss Veatch has pointed out:

The difference lies in the *instructional* role of the teacher. For example, in recreational reading we find the following: a weekly or bi-weekly period; little or no actual instruction; teacher largely inactive and free once books are chosen; little attention to skill development; reading entirely silent.

A quite different picture is found in the individualized approach, to wit: a daily reading period; continual instruction; teacher active and in demand; concern for skill development; reading silent with frequent opportunities to read orally to the teacher and to the class.[30]

As a result of their observations in a variety of classroom situations where they watched individualized reading programs in operation under the supervision of many kinds of teachers, Peggy Brogan and Lorene Fox developed a number of concepts and assumptions which they felt were common to the methodology of most of the individualized reading programs they saw:

Children need to read.

Individual children vary widely in their ways of approaching reading.

There is no one best way for organizing the individual reading of books by children in the classroom.

Teachers must give children the particular kind of help that they need to learn to read.

Children need to feel good about themselves and reading.

Children need opportunity to read uninterruptedly from books they can read.

Children need sensitive friendly help available—to be told the words they do not know.

Help in analysis of words can be more useful to children at other times of day, when it does not interrupt the story or content.

Children need opportunity to select from a variety of good books from the beginning.

The more of the reading period individual children spend *reading*—not discussing and not listening to other children take turns reading—the better they are apt to read and to comprehend what they are reading.

Word drills, motivation discussions, other step-by-step group procedures at the time of story or book reading are sure to be a waste of time for many children.

Teachers and administrators should accept the fact that children of the same age differ widely in reading ability.

Expectations that all children in a class will or should read at the narrowly defined grade-level are unscientific, unrealistic, and unfair to children. It is the expectations, not the children, that are at fault that they do not come up to the norm or above.

Every child should be genuinely accepted and respected as and where he is in reading and helped to go on from there.

Teachers do not have to give children tests to find out where they are in reading. Opportunity for them to select from a good variety of books those which they can find they can read, will give the teacher much more reliable information about her individual children and their reading.

The opportunity to read uninterruptedly from a choice of books he can read and enjoy is important for children, not only in elementary school, but on up through junior and senior high school as well. Their range of abilities and interests in reading will naturally grow wider as the children grow older.[31]

The individualized method of reading instruction is, then, quite clearly a way of thinking about reading which is based on an attempt to provide for individual differences while at the same time recognizing interest and purpose as prime factors in the learning process. It is designed to allow the child to develop his own unique direction and pace rather than to fit him into a prescribed mode of development supposed typical or normal for his age group. It makes provision for reading activities which develop the needed reading skills in functional settings, capitalizes upon opportunities for the development of skills in other areas of the curriculum and throughout the school day, and recognizes the interrelationship of all of the language arts—speaking, listening, reading, and writing—which are based on a wide variety of interesting experiences closely related to the real activities and interests in the child's life that provide entries into learning situations.

Writing of the plan that she did so much to foster, Jeannette Veatch said:

Briefly this new reading program is based upon the idea that children can and do read better, more widely and with vastly increased interest, when allowed to choose their own reading materials.

This, it is clear, is in direct opposition to basal reading programs, although it does not exclude the books used in basal reading programs. The self-selection principle discards the well known idea of planned sequential development of level of difficulty programs of basal readers. . . .

In summation, it is interesting to note the extent of development of such a program throughout the country. It seems that a spontaneous development has taken place in widely separated geographic areas without the individuals concerned realizing that there was a similar development elsewhere. It is also interesting to note that the specialized field of reading has undeniably been taken unawares, as all major writing in this area has come from educators more recognized for their general curriculum interests than for specialization in reading.[32]

While among the various writers in the field there are minor variations in the procedural recommendations for setting up and operating the individualized reading program in the middle grades of the elementary school, a consideration of the methodology of individualized reading ordinarily involves five basic elements:

1. The materials of instruction.

2. The organization of the classroom.

3. Reading conferences and reading records.

4. Related instructional and creative activities.

5. The evaluation of children's growth in reading

The succeeding five chapters will deal with each of these elements of the program; first, from the point of view of describing the underlying philosophy and operational procedure, and secondly, from the point of view of the implications that each of these elements holds for the elementary-school librarian.

III. THE MATERIALS OF INSTRUCTION

One of the most important characteristics of the individualized reading program is the utilization of a wide variety of trade and text books for the purpose of instruction, rather than relying on a basic reading textbook. In fact, it may well be that the individualized reading program is, at least in part, the result of technological advances in the publishing industry which have made a tremendous assortment of children's books available in remarkably attractive formats that are reasonably inexpensive. The books for children which are so readily available today on every conceivable subject and on a wide range of reading levels are often so imaginatively produced that they offer a built-in motivational factor. Basic to the individualized reading plan is the availability of an adequate number of trade and textbooks which represents a wide range of reading interests and levels of reading difficulty and from which the child can freely choose the materials that he wants to read.

Since the methodology of individualized reading is based, in part, on the theories of Willard Olson, the importance of the child's free choice of materials is strongly emphasized in the program. The philosophy of the method maintains that when a child chooses for himself the book he wants to read he is engaged in an act of self-expression that can have a powerful influence on his attitude towards reading and on the meaning that he will derive from the reading experience itself. While some children seem to demonstrate an unusual knack for choosing books within their range of reading ability, they still need a good deal of guidance in book selection from teachers and librarians. Children become more competent and effective in exercising their freedom of choice as knowledge of their interests and abilities is made clearer to them and as the nature and content of available reading materials is revealed to them by professional personnel.

DETERMINING INTERESTS AND NEEDS

Several significant studies have been made of children's interests which are useful to librarians and teachers in making book selection decisions and in performing reading guidance functions. Two of the most recently completed studies, one by Harlan Shores and Herbert Rudman[33] and the other by George Norvell,[34] shed new light on important factors of reading guidance. The former study analyzes responses on over eleven thousand questionnaires from children in grades four through eight, their parents, teachers, and librarians. Among the generalizations the authors develop about the children's reading interests are that children have similar reading interests regardless of where they live—city, country, or suburbs—and that there are really few significant differences between the reading interests of boys and girls. They conclude that science is an area of prime interest and concern among children, that children want action and adventure books at all grade levels studied, and that there is no significant relationship between the subjects which children ask about and look up in reference books and the subjects about which they choose to read a book. While George Norvell's study disagrees on the similarity of reading interests between boys and girls, many of his other findings are essentially in agreement with those of Shores and Rudman. He finds that in the eight- to twelve-year-old group, animal stories rank highest in popularity, followed quite closely by biography, and that when children of all ages and backgrounds and of both sexes are considered collectively, humor is the most enjoyed characteristic of their literature. Significantly, he can find no relationship between intelligence and choice of reading interests.

Helen Darrow and Virgil Howes have compiled a useful summary of the results of several other studies of children's reading interests conducted during the late forties and early fifties:

When children first begin to read they enjoy those stories based on familiar settings and experiences—pets, toys, other children like themselves. Further, they enjoy fairy tales; funny stories about people, animals, happenings; surprise and action stories; nonsense stories; rhymes and jingles. Early in the intermediate grades, adventure stories, biographies of great men and women, stories about people in other parts of the world, and imaginative stories about kings and queens are more frequently chosen; later, nature and science books, travel books, club and game stories, mystery and semi-fictional stories. By junior high school grades, reading interests are modified somewhat on the basis of sex. Girls favor human interest and romantic stories, whereas boys prefer informative or descriptive stories about inventions, machines, sports, and scientific problems.[35]

Since each child is unique and reading interests tend to change rather rapidly, proponents of individualized reading emphasize the importance of regularly appraising the changing pattern of interests among the children with whom a teacher or librarian is working. Probably the best day-to-day guide is personal observation of each child's expression of present or potential interest. Since the methodology of individualized reading instruction makes provision for regular conferences between individual children and the teacher, an opportunity is periodically available for discussions on a one-to-one basis of the child's favorite leisure-time activities, current interests and enthusiasms—pets, movies, and television programs—long-range career interests and ambitions, and previous reading experiences, all of which offer useful clues to the child's interest profile and thus to potential areas of development through reading guidance. Nancy Larrick has suggested a list of questions that would be useful for the librarian's survey of individual interests or for administration by the classroom teacher at the beginning of the school year:

1. When do you have the most fun at home?
2. Why do you have a pet? Or why not?
3. What person do you like to play with best of all?
4. At school whom do you like to play with?
5. What do you like to play indoors?
6. What do you like to play outdoors?
7. What is your favorite sport?
8. What is your favorite hobby?
9. What is the one thing you want to learn more about?
10. What is the one thing you want to learn to make?
11. If you could do anything you please next Saturday, what would you do?
12. If your class could take a one-day trip, where would you like to go?
13. What is your favorite movie?
14. What is your favorite television program?
15. What is your next favorite television program?
16. What book have you enjoyed reading more than any other?
17. What do you like to read about?

animals   science   make-believe   nature
covered-wagon days   sports   knights of old
boys' adventures   trains and planes

18. What person (in real life or in history) do you want to be like?

Donald Durrell has developed a more detailed inventory which yields many clues to children's individual interests and aptitudes which are useful in reading guidance and in the development of correlations between reading experiences in the individualized program and other areas of the elementary-school program.[37]

Some writers have also suggested that the individualized reading program can make important contributions in meeting children's emotional needs.[38] It is difficult to measure the validity of many of the assumptions that are made about bibliotherapeutic techniques, within the design of controlled experimental studies, because of the lack of adequate measuring devices and the great number of variables which are involved in undertakings that aim to affect emotional changes. However, many teachers and librarians feel that books and stories frequently play an important role in helping children to solve, or at least to rationalize, personal and social adjustment problems through the way that they help them to gain insight into difficult situations or to relieve feelings of fear or guilt. Virgil Howes has suggested several techniques which may be used jointly by teachers and librarians to develop clues to children's personality needs for use in reading guidance:

The Wish Test.—Each child is asked to make a specified number of wishes about home, school, play, people, or about himself. These are analyzed for clues about problems the child may be facing, desires, fears, and other valuable information about the way he sees his world.

Incomplete Sentence Inventory.—Children frequently make revealing statements about themselves and their feelings when asked to complete a sentence with familiar beginning words supplied by the teacher. Examples like the following can be used:

- Sometimes I dislike...................
  I like................................
- I work best when ....
  My favorite story ....
- Reading ....
  The library ....
- I get mad when ....

Autobiographies.—With young children a good technique is to have each child make a book about himself. In this he can include stories and pictures of himself, father, mother, pets, friends, toys, home, and so on. Pictures can be photographs or perhaps pictures cut from magazines to represent various things in his life. Older children can write their autobiographies. Some times an outline will help them to make a complete story. This might be cooperatively developed by the class or the teacher might suggest topics such as:

My Life Before I Started School
My Elementary School Days
My Home
My Friends
My Interests and Hobbies
My Future

Picture Story.—Students bring a picture, draw a picture, or use one provided by the teacher as a basis for a written or oral story. They include in the story such things as what has happened, how do the people feel, what are they doing, and how does it end. Information from these stories will often provide valuable insights into the child's world, his feelings, and his needs.[39]

DETERMINING CHILDREN'S READING LEVEL

In addition to the determination of children's individual interests and needs, a third factor which is involved in book selection and reading guidance in the individualized reading program is reading level. Individualized reading is an attempt to meet the wide range of individual differences in reading ability which exists in the typical elementary-school classroom. It has been said that a criterion of good teaching in a given elementary-school situation is the growing divergence in the range of abilities of a group of children as they move through the grades so that by the sixth grade there may well be a spread of ten or more years among the children in terms of their reading abilities. Such a range in individual abilities must obviously be an important consideration in the selection of reading materials for any class group, especially one in the middle grades.

When children take a standardized reading test, the raw scores that they earn are usually converted into graded reading-level equivalents. The relationship between raw scores and reading grade levels is derived from a statistical standardization process which all reputable authors of achievement tests utilize in the construction of their instruments. This process involves administering the tests to large numbers of students who are representative of the general population of children who will be taking the test in its final form. Thus, when a given class takes a standardized reading achievement test in the second month of the fifth grade, it is anticipated that the child who earns the median score in the group will probably be at a reading-level equivalent to approximately 5.2 (fifth grade, second month), that half of the class will earn scores ranging upward from 5.2, and that the other half of the class will earn scores ranging downward from 5.2, though, of course, the majority of the class members will be clustered around the 5.2 level. Thus, in a typical heterogeneous fifth-grade class of thirty pupils, the results of a reading achievement test taken in October might look like Table I.

Table I.

Range of Reading Achievement	Number of Pupils
1.0 - 1.9	1
2.0 - 2.9	1
3.0 - 3.9	2
4.0 - 4.9	7
5.0 - 5.9	11
6.0 - 6.9	5
7.0 - 7.9	1
8.0 - 8.9	1
9.0 - 9.9	1

Useful as such tests are in helping a teacher or librarian to characterize the range and distribution of abilities in a group of children, the scores, when applied to individuals, are limited in value. First of all, the scores expressed as

grade-level equivalencies are often misinter-
preted. When a child taking a test in the second
month of the fifth grade earns a grade-level score
of 4.2, it does not necessarily mean that he can
only read early fourth-grade-level materials;
rather, it means that he did as well on the material comprising the test as the child who received the median score when taking the test in
the second month of his fourth grade during the
standardization procedure. It must also be re-
membered that the score that a given child re-
ceives on a reading test is greatly influenced by a
number of variable factors: by the interest that
the child has in the particular material that is
included in the test, by how closely the reading
material used for testing relates to his own personal real-life experiences, by how well the child
reacts emotionally to testing situations, and by
his physical condition at the time of testing.
Aside from the fact that what standardized tests
tell us may be misleading, they do not tell us a
number of things that are extremely important
in determining a child's ability to read a given
book. They fail to tell how much the child may
want to read on specific subjects in which high
motivation may make it possible for him to read
effectively far above his usual level; they fail to
tell us how widely he reads on his own; and they
fail to tell us whether he is developing taste and

discrimination in his selection of reading materials. Yet today in modern education—in the typical elementary school—great reliance is often placed on the results of standardized reading achievement tests. In the ability-grouped basal reading type of instructional program, children are often placed in reading groups solely on the basis of the scores they have made on such tests, and in some schools children may be retained in a grade for an additional year, because they failed to make a satisfactory score on a reading test.

Walter Barbe has commented that each child, in reality, has many reading levels upon which he functions, depending on a variety of factors, and that even this complex of reading levels may fluctuate to a considerable degree from day to day:

Teachers must remember that the reading level is not rigidly set and that it may be influenced by many factors. Understanding this flexibility of the reading level makes the need for a flexible type of reading instructional program even more apparent. It is true that there may be freedom of movement between ability groups in the basal reader approach, although there is great question as to how a child in one level can ever actually get to the next level, if by the time he has learned to read as well as the children in the next group, they have moved on to a higher level.   In the personalized reading program, such grouping problems do not arise, since the only grouping is of a temporary nature for a specific purpose and is disbanded as soon as the purpose is accomplished.

The need is not so much for a definite reading level for each child, which can be recorded on a test or record blank, but in-

stead there is a need for an approximation of reading level
in each of a variety of reading skills . . . . The important thing
to remember is that a reading level score is only an indication of
what the child is actually achieving. The teacher's responsibility is to aid the child in learning to read material beyond
this point. To the extent that she does this, along with developing the desire to read these materials, she will be successful as a
teacher of reading.[40]

Dr. Barbe suggests that the most useful tests of
reading are not those that simply measure reading achievement or place the child at a theoretical reading-grade level, but rather diagnostic
reading tests. Standardized reading achievement
tests ordinarily measure only two areas involved
in the total reading picture: word meaning and
sentence or paragraph comprehension. Diagnostic reading tests are not so concerned with assign-
ing a grade-level score to a child as they are with
revealing precisely where and why a child is having difficulty in reading. Such tests are of great
value in the individualized reading program, because the information they reveal about specific
difficulties and weaknesses can be used by
the teacher in helping him to decide what type
of special-purpose, short-duration instructional
grouping may be needed for specific groups of
children. Diagnostic test results may reveal, for
instance, that difficulty in comprehension arises
from lack of understanding of word meanings,
lack of ability in phrasing, need for guidance
in recognizing main ideas, and so forth. Dif-

ficulty with word analysis may be revealed as arising from the need for additional instruction in letter sounds, consonant blends, syllabication, or accenting. The flexibility of the individualized reading program then enables the teacher to make provision for instruction when and where it is needed.

The individualized reading conferences between the teacher and the student also afford regular opportunities to approximate the child's ability in reading from week to week. These are necessary if only because of the need to know what types of material a child may be ready to cope with when dealing with his reading guidance. Reading level may be rapidly approximated by having the child read silently and then orally a brief excerpt from an appropriate level of a basic reader. If the material proves to be too difficult, the book from the next lower reading level is tried; if it proves to be too easy, the book from the next higher level is used. When reading is obviously too slow or labored, or if the child has difficulty with more than three words on a page, the book is considered to be too difficult. The results of these periodic evaluations need to be shared by teachers and librarians and their implications analyzed in planning effective reading guidance procedures for the child.

ANTICIPATING DEMAND FOR MATERIALS

Willard Olson, as part of the work in which he correlated his theories of seeking, self-selection, and pacing with reading instruction, developed a useful index indicating the percentage of children at each grade level of elementary school that will be ready for books at a given grade and age level of reading difficulty. The index is based on the assumptions that children must be at least five years old before entering kindergarten and that promotion is more or less automatic each year. It indicates both the wide range of reading abilities in each grade and the tendency of this range of abilities to widen as children move through the elementary school.

Table II.
Percentage of Children in Each Grade
Ready for Each Book Level[41]

Book Level		Grade Level (*in percent*)					
Grade	*Age*	I	II	III	IV	V	VI
N. S.	5	2	2	2			
Kgn.	6	23	8	5	7		
1	7	50	24	11	9	7	
2	8	23	33	20	10	9	7
3	9	2	24	24	16	10	9
4	10		8	20	17	16	10
5	11		2	11	16	17	16
6	12			5	10	16	17
7	13			2	9	10	16
8	14				7	9	10
9	15					7	9
10	16						7

The information summarized on Table II has important implications for the teacher and the librarian in their anticipation of the basic book needs of a typical elementary-school classroom. The chart indicates these needs at approximately midyear for each of the six grade levels. It may be seen, for instance, that at the fourth-grade level only 17 percent of the children in such a class will need materials at that level of difficulty with the remainder of the children requiring materials either above or below that level of difficulty. From the standpoint of the total school collection, the greatest demand will be placed on books of the second- and third-grade levels of reading difficulty. Examination of the data on the chart also reveals that while in the middle of first grade 50 percent of the children will need materials at that grade level of difficulty, only 33 percent of the children in second grade will be requiring materials at their grade level of reading difficulty, and this figure drops to 24 percent in third grade and to 17 percent in fourth grade. This trend seems to reflect the belief of individualized reading proponents that the longer children are exposed to situations where they have an opportunity to read, the more unlike they will become in their ability to do so. Teachers and librarians who use this or similar guides in developing book collections need to bear in mind that children who are significantly above grade level in reading ability can and do read a great deal more, in terms of quantity, than those at or below grade level in reading ability; thus, the needs at upper levels of reading difficulty, again in terms of numbers of books, are probably greater than the percentages indicate.

QUALITY FACTORS IN BOOK SELECTION

Children's interests and personal needs as well as their levels of reading ability play an important part in determining the kind and quantity of reading materials that will be needed to implement a successful individualized reading program. When needs are known in terms of these factors, quality, of course, plays a key role in the determination of actual titles by teachers and librarians. Lists of criteria for judging quality in children's books are numerous, but the problem is a complex one, for what will arouse avid enthusiasm in an adult will often fail to stimulate a child or win his approval. Paul Hazard, in his classic work on children's literature, offers the admonition that,

Children defend themselves. . . . They manifest at first a degree of inertia that resists the liveliest attacks; finally they take the offensive and expel their false friends from a domain in which they wish to remain the rulers. Nothing is done to create a common opinion among them and yet that opinion exists. They would be wholly incapable of defining the faults that displease them; but they cannot be made to believe that a book which displeases them should please them. . . . The adults insist, the children pretend to yield, and do not yield. We overpower them; they rise up again. Thus does the struggle continue, in which the weaker will triumph.[42]

In his summation of a detailed study of the reading interests and tastes of boys and girls, George Norvell advises teachers and librarians to reject completely the advice of authorities and that they consult their own tastes when selecting books for children. He reminds those responsible for book selection that *Tom Sawyer, Huckleberry Finn,* and *Treasure Island* were once labeled by authorities as dangerous and trashy and that the same thing will undoubtedly happen again.[43]

William Burton, Clara Baker, and Grace Kemp have suggested a list of criteria for evaluating quality in children's books that seems flexible and permissive enough to lend itself to the aims and objectives of the philosophy of individualized reading programs:

1. Interesting and vivid.—The materials must appeal to the typical known interests of children . . . be vividly presented without sacrifice of literary values.

2. Useful and purposeful—The materials must help children:

a. to expand their experiences, understand better the physical world in which they live.

b. to solve their personal problems or to obtain pleasure and enjoyment.

c. to develop appropriate creative abilities.

3.Truthful and honest—If the materials include real life content, as travel stories, historical writings, biographical themes, scientific materials, they must be objectively accurate from the standpoint of facts. If they include fictional content of a realistic nature, they must be honest in the portrayal of human life and action, objectively possible in activities and outcomes. If they include make-believe or exaggerated content, as fanciful stories, tall tales, nonsense items, they must possess enough credibility to make them seem possible.

4. Meaningful to the reader.—The concepts and vocabulary must be suited to the reader's maturity, experience background, and educational development.

5. Effectively written.—The language must be competent in terms of correct usage and vividness of style . . . appropriate to the reader's ability to read and understand. It must introduce humor, nonsense, and fancy without using odd, bizarre, extreme, and unlikely devices.

6. Well-illustrated, attractively bound, and of good format.—The illustrations must help to stimulate interest in, and to strengthen comprehension of, the materials.

7. As wide as life itself in range.—Giving numerous, varied, and vivid opportunities for vicarious experiencing.[44]

Observing that, "A book may be considered a juvenile classic by the experts, but if it is beyond the child's understanding or too subtle or precocious for his level of appreciation, he can turn it down with a stony indifference which leaves adults baffled and grieved," May Arbuthnot offers two sets of criteria for children's book selection, one for story books and the other for informational books. Of story books she writes,

Of course, a child's reading will not and should not be limited to stories, but stories are his first and most lasting literary love. He hears them with delight at three and will probably enjoy them throughout adolesence and maturity. What are the distinguishing characteristics of a well-written story? In general, children like stories with an *adequate theme*, strong enough to generate and support a *lively plot*. They appreciate *memorable characters* and *distinctive style*. Most stories which have become durable additions to children's literature have had these characteristics.[45]

Miss Arbuthnot then proceeds to examine each of these elements—theme, plot, characters, and style—in considerable detail. Of informational books she comments that:

The best we can do here is to set up criteria for judging these books on the basis of scrupulous accuracy (unless our text is accurate our reading is worse than useless; accuracy is the most important criterion for judging any informational book), convenient presentation (we want the material presented in such a way that we can find what we are looking for quickly and comfortably; this is equally true of children), clarity (information for any age level should be written directly and sensibly, with obvious respect for the reader's intelligence) adequate treatment (it is essential that enough significant facts be given for a realistic and balanced picture), and style (a lively, well-written text is an invaluable bait to learning.).[46]

IMPLICATIONS FOR LIBRARIANS

The elementary-school librarian's role in implementing the program of individualized reading in the area of the materials of instruction is fundamental to the program's success. It is obvious that his knowledge of children's reading materials can be of inestimable value to teachers and children. There are, however, certain facets of his role in reading guidance which are modified somewhat by the nature of individualized reading's theory and philosophy. There is, for instance, the paradox that the methodology of individualized reading is based on the concept of complete freedom of choice by the child in the selection of materials to be read, while at the same time the variety of materials used in the program demands a great deal more reading guidance than does the traditional type of basal reading program. The implication seems to be that guidance in individualized programs must be subtle rather than direct, that is, that the librarians must work to create a readiness in children so that they can exercise wisdom in choosing their reading materials.

Children do not always choose books on their reading level; they may have specific and very important reasons for choosing books which are above or below the level of difficulty at which they can read with profit and understanding. There are times when even the ablest of readers will choose something extremely easy to read, perhaps simply to revisit some favorite story characters or situations or because the format and illustrations of a book appeal to him. Children will sometimes choose very difficult materials, particularly nonfiction, if they have been strongly motivated to develop information in some area of investigation. There are, of course, situations where inappropriate choices of reading materials are made that need thoughtful intervention by the librarian. Excessive book-report requirements or factual textbook readings in the classroom may underlie a child's tendency to choose easy books to read; sometimes such choices by a child may result from his lack of courage or fear of failure in working with more challenging materials. The librarian who notes such patterns of selection needs to work cooperatively with the teacher to plan ways of helping the children involved to recognize their own abilities and strengthen their self-confidence. Children who consistently choose books that are too difficult for them may be reacting to competition, home pressures, imitation, or overstimulation from parents or teachers. The librarian needs to exercise great tact in helping the weak reader find something that he can read with profit and that will also satisfy him and enable him to rationalize the pressures that may be acting upon him.

Beyond dealing with these common problems that may arise when children are permitted the freedom of seeking and self-selection in the choice of their reading materials, the librarian acts as the educational or informational force that makes wise self-selection possible. The success of individualized reading rests, in part, on the availability of a wide variety of reading materials which reflects a wide range of reading-difficulty levels and reading interests, but how well children exercise their freedom of choice depends

greatly on how much they know about the materials that are at their disposal, that is, on how
efficiently the collection of reading materials has
been introduced to them. Nancy Larrick has examined this relationship between the exercise
of free choice and the child's knowledge of materials as it specifically relates to the role of
librarians:

If the librarian has been able to introduce certain books to
one class through storytelling, reading aloud, or capsule summary she has alerted those youngsters to the possibility of those
particular books. If she has displayed the jackets or perhaps
children's evaluations of the books, she may be able to reach
still more of the youngsters. If she has given teachers an opportunity to explore new books, she may be able to enlist their
support in advertising her wares. And because they know something of the books in advance, children will be able to make
their selections more easily and more effectively.[47]

In the process of book selection, librarians must
bear in mind the realities of reading abilities as
they exist in the particular schools that they
serve. In the daily activities of reading guidance,
the breadth of the range in abilities is of prime
importance to the librarian's work with individual children. Dr. Olson has pointed out that
in the typical heterogeneous sixth-grade classroom the abilities of individual children may
range from the second- to the tenth-grade reading levels.

Librarians need to keep alert to new findings
in the field of children's interests and needs, par-

ticularly as the findings relate to reading guidance. The recent extensive study by George Norvell of the reading patterns and preferences of 24,000 children in grades three through six is an example of the type of continuing research which sheds light on significant aspects of reading guidance.   Regarding the choice of materials for and by children, Dr. Norvell found, for instance, that:

1. Reading materials for children have an excellent chance for popularity when they combine several of the favorable interest factors—action, humor, animals, patriotism, holidays—and are free of the unfavorable—nature (poetry of trees, flowers, birds, bees), didacticism, fairies.

2. Children approve or disapprove individual selections regardless of authorship.

3. When told as adventure, biography is popular with both boys and girls.

4. The prose selection which fails to tell an adventurous story is unlikely to meet with children's approval.

5. Superior, average, and slow pupils usually enjoy the same kinds of reading materials.

6. Encourage and guide each child to follow his own reading bent.

7. Reject completely the advice, "Consult your own taste," and enjoy the selection through the pleasure of boys and girls[48]

The findings of this important study support some of the most basic principles regarding the use of materials in the individualized reading program: that the reading habit is based on a love of reading and that the development of this attitude is the most important academic aim of the elementary school; that every activity requiring reading should be appraised in the light of this aim; and that reading should be indulged in to the point where the reader is unconscious of effort. "An appalling number of non-readers among adults," writes Dr. Norvell, "fail to read because they never reached the stage when the reading of even simple material ceased to be an irksome struggle." He suggests that provision for a vast amount of pleasurable reading experiences in school is the answer. Essentially, this is the major aim of reading guidance in the individualized reading program.

IV. THE ORGANIZATION OF THE CLASSROOM

INITIATING THE PROGRAM

An analysis of thirty-two articles written by classroom teachers about their experiences in teaching by individualized reading, which appeared in educational periodicals between 1952 and 1962, reveals the following information about their initiation of the program:

1. All the teachers had been using the ability-grouped basal reading method of instruction prior to their experimentation with the individualized approach.

2. Of the twenty-eight teachers who reported where they had first heard of individualized reading or received encouragement to try it out, nineteen attributed their initial orientation to material they had found in educational books and magazines on the subject, six had heard about it from professors at colleges and universities, and three had received advice and encouragement from administrative personnel in the schools where they taught.

3. About half the teachers who reported how they got started with the program in the classroom said that they had begun with the usual

three ability groups in the basal reading program and had individualized either the highest or lowest reading group first, later moving the rest of the class into the program. The remainder of the teachers reported moving the entire class into the program simultaneously.

Typical of these teachers' reports of their experiences with individualized reading instruction is one written by Mary Ann Daniel, a fifth-grade teacher in Abingdon, Pennsylvania:

> Recently, many articles have been written stressing the effectiveness of individualized reading programs. I became as enthusiastic as anyone else who had read these articles—here at last was a method which could cope with the wide range of reading abilities in the classroom. . . .
> As I gazed at the 36 faces—some eager, some apprehensive —on the first day of school in September, I wondered if my plan would succeed, It sounded perfect in every article I read. But 36 fifth-grade youngsters! My school district, in a rather well-to-do suburb of Philadelphia, believes in grouping for reading. Almost every classroom in our eleven elementary schools has three ability groups. This year, a new reading series was purchased which encouraged the ability grouping. The size of my class and the policy of the school district would certainly encourage the old-fashioned ability grouping![49]

Determined to work out a plan wherein she could combine basal and individualized reading instruction, Miss Daniel, describes how she developed her three ability groups. She gradually established a policy, for the highest group first, that one day a week they could read any book they selected during the reading program. The program was expanded gradually to include the other two reading groups and a greater proportion of the reading periods. She concludes:

As I have watched this reading program develop since September, I have been most pleased with the results. It has enabled me to know more about the level and ability of each child. Thus I have been able to give more worth-while individual and group instruction. Naturally, as the children read more books, they became more skilled in self-selection of books. They are very capable of selecting books that they understand and that are well-written. The weaker pupils are not embarrassed by their selection of easier books, and the superior readers are not held back. Everyone exhibits more enthusiasm and interest in reading. . . . [50]

Reporting on her experiences with a fourth grade class in a somewhat more permissive school setting, Phyllis Parkin writes:

At the very beginning of the year, before any type of program was under way, she told the children that this year reading was going to be different. She explained that there would be no reading groups as such and that each person would choose his own book and read it as he was able. She talked with the pupils about choosing carefully and planning to finish the book begun. She also told them not to return a book that looked easy because in doing so they might cheat themselves of a good story. (This suggestion was made with the idea of lifting pressure from the slow reader who needed to choose an easy book to read.)

The teacher further explained that, instead of calling groups of children to read with her every day, she would stop by to talk with each child about the book he was reading or to ask him to read to her. She would always be present to answer questions or to help in finding a book. From time to time, she would bring together children who needed the same kind of help and work with them in a group; this group would not remain the same, though, from one day to the next. [51]

Miss Parkin spent considerable time at the beginning of the school year orienting the children in her class to individualized reading routines. One day, early in the term, she asked the children if they thought it would be a good idea to keep records of the books that they were reading so that by the end of the year they could see what they had accomplished. She worked together with the children to develop cooperatively various procedures that could be followed during the daily reading periods. As the children made suggestions, she wrote the following activities on the board:

1. Choose a book to read.
2. Read.
3. List the book in your notebook.
4. Read together.
5. List new words and their meanings.
6. Share the books that you read.
7. Do something with what you read.[52]

When the children in the classroom are supplied with books that reflect their interests, needs and range of reading abilities, one of the greatest problems in reading instruction—motivating the children to want to read—is all but solved. With the right collection of books on hand, the teacher and the librarian need not motivate children to read in the overt salesman-like way which is often recommended by the proponents of basal reading instruction. The teacher so prepared with materials, or the school librarian who works with children and the teacher, acts rather, as Jeannette Veatch has written, like a catalyst designed to bring children and books together in an atmosphere which permits freedom to browse and to select. Children read what they want to read, and they learn to improve their reading skills and tastes by the reading experience itself.

Most writers agree that there is no single approach to the teaching of reading the individualized way but rather that individualized reading is based on a way of thinking that involves new concepts of classroom organization and instructional techniques. Other writers have said that there are as many ways of organizing the classroom program for reading instruction as there are teachers of individualized reading. However, a survey of educational literature indicates that, while there are indeed numerous variations and approaches reported, individualized reading programs as they are described in practice do have certain fundamental characteristics in common:

1. The basic principles established by Willard Olson in 1949 regarding seeking and self-selection by the child and pacing by the teacher are intrinsic parts of the program.

2. Provision is always made for individual reading conferences between the children and

the teacher to discuss each child's book in progress.

3. Groups are organized from time to time for a variety of reasons, sometimes for instructional purposes, but also quite often for purposes of a social or creative nature.

4. The children play an important role in stimulating other children in the class to read through the sharing of their reading experiences with the classroom group. Children appear to accept recommendations from their peers more readily than they do from adults.

FROM DAY TO DAY

If librarians are to enter into an effective partnership with teachers in the individualized reading program, it is undoubtedly important for them to be aware of exactly what form the reading instruction takes in the classroom during the daily periods. They can, of course, gather this information through conferences with teachers or requests to visit classrooms during reading periods. An attempt will be made here to describe what might typically be taking place in terms of time allotments and teaching activities.

Most of the educators who have contributed to the literature on individualized reading have stressed the importance of prethinking and preplanning by the teacher; these activities are no less important in individualized reading programs than they are in basal reading programs. These writers have, however, avoided any mention of exactly how much time should be spent on reading each day or any prescription of what activities should take place during the individualized reading periods. Writers who have suggested flexible frameworks for the periods do advise teachers to allow adequate time to develop a strong program and do include such recommended activities as book selection, reading conferences, creative and instructional activities related to reading experiences, and the sharing of these experiences with the class group.

Alvina Burrows did much to foster what she and a number of her colleagues felt had to be a new kind of teacher planning which would be distinctly different from the traditional type of day-to-day group assignments, different because those teachers who approach a classroom of children as individuals cannot think, write, and plan in terms of a combined group. Beginning with the premise that any plan for individualized instruction must be flexible and fluid, while still providing continuity and variety of activities, Dr. Burrows developed a weekly pattern that was influential in determining the approach and procedures used by many teachers who individualized their reading instruction:

In a few minutes at the beginning of each reading period a check is made to discover who needs new material, who needs the teacher's help, or who needs to get books from the library. Such a brief planning session saves time later. Perhaps five or ten minutes will be enough to get the group started.

Monday.—Teacher invites children reading "very hard books" to sit near her for help with words. To include strong and weak readers in such a group improves morale. Each reads a book of his own selection. Some children may be able to read only 10-20 minutes depending upon attention span.

Teacher has individual reading conferences with two or three pupils.

Most of the group read silently by themselves in books self-chosen or assigned by teacher while teacher works with individuals or groups. Content may be informational or fictional. Some may be related to content unit; most reading will be more personal. Storybooks, magazines, textbooks are a few of the varied reading sources.

Tuesday.—Another opportunity for individual help on hard reading will include some of the same children who were in the group Monday. Working two days in succession with individuals who are weak readers often seems more helpful than at longer intervals.

Three or four individual conferences. Children sign on blackboard when they want a conference or at teacher's request.

Most of the group read silently as individuals. No formal checking on individuals.

Wednesday.—About half an hour for talking about books or for dramatization, reading aloud, informal chatting about favorite books, sharing of illustrations.

Two or three individual conferences before the group discussion or, if needed, to prepare a bit of oral reading, or to check plan with teacher.

Thursday.—Conferences with six or seven individuals while most of group read independently. Some may do occasional assignments if need is shown for particular reading.

Most of the children read individually. Weak readers must also have opportunity to choose some of their reading.

Encourage some individuals to prepare a section which has been read to teacher as preparation for oral reading to the class, or to a small group.

Friday.—Pupils bring reading records up to date. Teacher checks on spelling and mechanics of book records.

Conferences with four or five individuals.

Most of the children read individually. Some get books for weekend reading at home.[53]

Dr. Burrows notes that provision should be made at the end of each day's reading period for a brief concluding meeting with the entire class group to allow time for children to comment on any very good stories or sections of books that they may have read during the period, for discussions of any problems that may have been encountered, or for talking over any related creative projects that may be in the planning stages. Such a concluding period may also be used by children who wish to give prepared dramatizations related to their readings, oral readings, or book talks.

Time allotments within such a framework are quite tentative. One conference may last three minutes while another may require ten minutes. Sometimes two or three children may work simultaneously with the teacher with profit for all. If a schedule of appointments cannot be kept for a certain day, the teacher may decide to move around the room and hear several children read for a few minutes, or he may ask several of the children to simply tell the name of the book that they are presently reading and what has just happened in the story. "Timing of the whole reading period," the author comments, "varies with maturity, fatigue, and other factors. Sometimes children can read with attention for only twenty minutes. It is important to stop when interest fails."[54]

One teacher, who kept a log of his activities during individualized reading periods, presents a picture of the kind of things that the teacher might be doing while silent reading is in progress by most of the children:

Monday.—All children read individually.   Worked with May, Tom . . . on comprehension—had group read and discuss selections. . . .   Held reading conferences with Joe, Sara, June.

Tuesday.—Worked with Susan, John . . . on double vowel sounds. Helped small group planning for St. Valentine's Day with their play to be shared with class. Other children worked on independent activities or read individually. Had reading conferences with. . . .

Wednesday.—Taught proper nouns to the children using book 2. Helped Carl prepare a story to read to the class. Had conferences with. . . .

Thursday.—Had children read to each other in small groups while I circulated; each child kept records of unfamiliar words. Had Tom, Larry, and Ella read orally to the class. Worked with small groups on dictionary skills.   Helped several   children work on creative activities.

Friday.—Worked with group of eight children on word recognition—asked them to make a list of 'r' words. Had class evaluate the week's reading.[55]

The librarian who is unfamiliar with the methodology of individualized reading as it takes daily form within the classroom would, if he were to observe a program in action, probably be most impressed at first with the variety of activities that often take place simultaneously. A group of children—perhaps five or six—might be busy in one corner of the room preparing a dramatization of a scene or a section from a book or story they have all read, another group might be working on a reading skill exercise previously assigned to them by the teacher, who noted during individual conferences that they shared a common need for practice in some reading skill, two or three other children might be working on a chart, map, or mural related either to common reading experiences or to a unit of work in science or social studies. Perhaps half the class might be reading silently in books of their own choice. The teacher may be engaged in a reading conference with one of the children, or he may be working on a reading skill with a small group. As has been noted, periods like this usually begin with a planning session in which the entire class participates, and they end with a sharing period which summarizes experiences and develops future plans.

The methodology of individualized reading creates a kind of atmosphere in the classroom and a way of working and living with children that has a way of permeating other areas of the curriculum and influencing the conduct of most of the school day. Actually, of course, many of the principles of individualization in reading instruction are applicable to other areas of the elementary-school curriculum, especially in the middle grades. Believing strongly in the principle of self-selection in learning, one teacher developed the following organizational plan:

Mr. Carlson's sixth-grade class begins the morning with Work Time, as they call it. A block of time of an hour and a half or two hours, this period is planned to include three kinds of activities in each of which every child is expected to participate, but in whatever order he may choose.

One of the three kinds of activities provided for, of course, is reading. . . . They may read a book to themselves or with a friend. Two or three may want to get copies of the same book and take turns in reading together. Several children may be reading in search of a story that will make a good play. A child may read to the teacher. Indeed this may well be the time when the teacher will want to work individually or with small groups informally set up. . . .

A second of the three parts . . . is given over to wider choices, individual and group. While others are reading, some children may be working on a play, painting scenery, making costumes, planning choreography. Others may be working with art media of various kinds, or with science materials, if that is what the job involves. Some may be working on a crossword puzzle to ditto for the class, or constructing a table game or a quiz board. . . .

The third type of activity. . . is usually some common assignment or jointly planned project for the total group, having to do with social studies, say, or science or arithmetic, or some other area of the curriculum. It may involve the use of teacher-made work sheets, usually a variety of them from which the children may select. It may be some aspect of research, the organizing of notes from references read, perhaps the making of plans for an interview, the recording of findings from a trip, some work on a chapter or story to contribute to one of the books which the class has under way. . . .

Mr. Carlson . . . feels that this kind of unpressured, informal responsible working together not only challenges children to thoughtful choice and action—a required condition for maximum growth in reading—it also gives the teacher a chance, on a good friendly basis, to work more closely with his children, to better observe their individual resources, and thus to give more appropriate encouragement and help.[56]

IMPLICATIONS FOR LIBRARIANS

A few years ago, when individualized reading was just getting its start as a method of instruction, many teachers turned to it out of a sense of frustration with ability-grouped basal reading instruction. The articles that they wrote in those formative years reveal that they made the transition in an almost secretive way with some misgiving about the fact they might be violating district policies in the school systems where they were employed. Today the situation has changed considerably. Despite attacks made on individualized reading by some of the proponents of basal reading instruction, the method has gained steadily in popularity and is being adopted in whole or in part by an increasing number of school systems. Undoubtedly, this trend is the result of a number of factors. Among these are the increased interest of educators in the kind of quality education that can only be achieved through some degree of individualization of instruction, the fact that a growing number of elementary schools are making provisions for a central library and the services of a professional librarian, and the encouraging results of accumulating evidence—the results of carefully controlled experimental studies—that individualized reading instruction is, in terms of the reading achievement of children, at least equal to ability-grouped basal reading instruction.

Today the role of the elementary-school librarian in the individualized reading program is likely to involve, first of all, the task of getting teachers—new teachers as well as those who have previously taught basal reading—started in the individualized program. The skilled librarian can do much to help teachers overcome feelings of insecurity that they may experience in approaching the new method. He can do this by providing them with the kinds of help that will contribute toward a feeling of confidence and the ability to think through for themselves the what and how of individualized instruction in reading. One of the principles of the method is that each teacher must develop his own patterns of classroom organization. To do this each teacher must evaluate his own feelings and attitudes, his own competencies, limitations, emotional needs, and skills in working with individuals. Such self-evaluation can be better achieved in the context of others' experiences with individualized reading programs. Since he is in touch with the various kinds of reading programs that are practiced in the school in which he serves, the librarian can often arrange fruitful sharing conferences between and among teachers where ideas and experiences in reading instruction may be exchanged. The librarian can also gather together various reading materials on the subject of individualized reading and make them available to interested teachers. Such educational periodicals as *Childhood Education*, *Elementary English*, and *The Reading Teacher* continue to publish articles and reports on new developments and programs in individualized reading. Several new books have come out which are entirely devoted to the subject. Many school systems have published handbooks and manuals on individualized reading in which they have interpreted the program's philosophy and methodology in terms of their local situations. Teachers College, Columbia University, has produced an excellent film, *Individualized Reading Instruction in the Classroom*, which is extremely useful in the graphic way that it shows teachers how the program might look in the reality of the classroom situation.

Those teachers who have made up their minds to individualize their reading programs and have thought through the organizational pattern that they feel they want to use will welcome help and suggestions from the librarian concerning materials, the process of self-selection, initial steps in the change-over to individualization, and the like. In the early operational stages of the program, the librarian will probably need to spend considerable time with the class involved in order to more thoroughly introduce the children to the range of possibilities for selection in the library and to assist the teacher in establishing the routines and patterns that he has decided to employ. Children need time to become adjusted to new organizational operations, and, if they have not had a good deal of previous experience in choosing books to read, they will need time to perfect their abilities to exercise self-selection. After the teacher and the librarian have shared the information that they have about the individual children who make up the class, they can work as a closely co-ordinated team in providing the needed reading guidance. In schools where individualized reading is widely practiced, the librarian might find it helpful to keep on file a brief description of the procedures that each teacher follows, since this will influence the way he works with each teacher's class during the course of the year.

Reports of individualized reading programs in action indicate that motivation among the children toward books and reading tends to build up rapidly. In the early stages of the program, information about books must come largely from the teacher and the librarian. Once the program is under way, however, children begin to stimulate each other with their own enthusiasms about the books and stories that they have enjoyed, and the desire to read specific selections becomes intrinsic rather than extrinsic in nature. The librarian can foster this tendency by applying what he has learned about children's interests and needs to the development of book talks, displays, and related programs and by making provision for time during library periods in which children may discuss their reading enthusiasms individually or in small panel discusssions planned in advance.

The classroom programs which were described earlier in the present chapter can obviously have a terrific impact on the way that the school library structures its own daily and weekly program. One of the best descriptions of how a school-wide change to individualized reading modified the concept and operations of the school library was provided recently by Jo Dewar, librarian at an elementary school in Fort Lauderdale, Florida. The program of library services that was developed to meet the demands of the new curriculum organization was the result of a series of conferences between the librarian and the instructional staff. The group examined the advantages and disadvantages of both the traditional and the more modern definitions of elementary-school library service and agreed on the concept of a free or open schedule of library operation. Under this plan, no entire class is scheduled for regular library periods except during orientation at the beginning of each school year and, in the case of the Fort Lauderdale school, story hours for first-grade children. It was decided to make the library available throughout the school day to every child in the school who had reason to come there.

Many activities go on simultaneously in our library. A primary group may be selecting books from the beginner shelf. A sixth-grade committee may be in the reference corner, working on plans for a solar stove. A teacher may be checking our filmstrip collection for material on South American Indians. These patrons can all be satisfied without interrupting a prearranged schedule. . . .

Personal attention can be given to the problems of reluctant readers or to the highly specialized requirements of advanced students. And Johnny Jones from the fourth-grade, who has just finished reading *King of the Wind* and wants another"neat" horse story, doesn't have to wait until next library day to satisfy his wishes.[57]

It may well be that in schools that practice individualized reading instruction it is advisable to keep the library schedule flexible and open-ended so that, while whole-class visits may be arranged whenever necessary, the library's facilities are always available to supplement whatever may be going on in the classrooms. Flexible scheduling makes it possible for the librarian to serve the right people at the right time: a research group in science or social studies, a special-purpose group sent down to the library by the teacher during the reading period, children who need individual reading guidance and who have simply come down to browse, a group of children planning some type of creative activity growing out of their reading experiences.

Regarding the problem of scheduling library visits, Jean Lowrie has suggested that it might be wise to reserve the first period each day for returning library books and the last period for browsing and to leave the remainder of the time entirely open to meet needs as they arise for individuals, small groups, and special-purpose visits by an entire class. She concludes:

> As the library experience ... becomes one of the basic ingredients in the teacher's daily classroom planning, it becomes less necessary for the librarian to pin down each class to a specific visit. Ergo, the less structured or tightly scheduled the library program is, the more comprehensive the service which it can give.[58]

The validity of these two hypotheses offered by Miss Lowrie seems indisputable. They are substantially reinforced in light of the advantages of individual instruction which have been cited by the proponents and practitioners of individualized reading. What these educators believe to

be true of reading skills and abilities is reflected
by Miss Dewar's evaluation of children's mastery
of library skills in the coordinated individualized
reading and library service program on which she
reported:

Our experiment with "freedom plus guidance" has the ear-
marks of success, at least. Inevitably, intangible results must
be judged empirically. From what we see, we can say that the
library is an integral part of every child's experience in our
school. Our children are more knowledgeable in library skills
because they have discovered individually what the library
can do for them.[59]

V. READING CONFERENCES
AND RECORDS

Regularly scheduled conferences between the teacher and the individual children in his class are a basic part of the methodology of all the programs of individualized reading that have been reported in the literature. Often the same techniques are used that librarians have employed in their reading guidance functions.

These short conferences usually begin with a friendly inquiry by the teacher regarding the nature or content of the book that the child is currently reading and has brought with him to the conference. This requires the child to give a brief descriptive summary of what has happened thus far in the book or story that he is reading. Such experiences in the demands of summation have definite advantages for the child. They give him the experience of selecting the most important and pertinent information; thus, he must be able to recognize and organize the main ideas of the material with which he is dealing. Such a task is, of course, difficult for the immature reader, and much guidance is often required by the teacher or the librarian in the process of selection. Much experience, however, in the relaxed conversational setting of the reading conference promotes growth in the child's ability to select only the most important ideas and consequently reject the unimportant detail. This is an important contribution to the child's growth in reading comprehension.

Jeannette Veatch has stressed the importance of the skillful use of open-ended questions during this phase of the conference:

Open-ended questions are those which are difficult to answer with a "yes" or "no" and require a bit of skill on the part of the teacher. For example, the question, "Did you like this story?" may bring either "Yes "or "No" as an answer. But to ask, "What kind of a story is this?" should bring a response that cannot so easily be encompassed in one word. This kind of question produces better teaching results because the answer gives you more information about the pupil's reading and allows the child to "talk out" — and thereby "think out"—his reactions.

Open-ended questions tend to bring forth information with little or no prodding or probing by the teacher. Compare these two questions and their possible answers:

1. "Show me the page where so-and-so did thus-and-so."
2. "Why do you think so-and-so is a funny character in this story?"

In the first question, the pupil would show the page requested and the question would be answered. Not so in the second question where the pupil might indicate several instances to document his answer to the question. The very nature of the second question requires much more information and much more thought than is the case with the first.[60]

In structuring the wording of questions, the teacher and the librarian who support this aspect of the program through contacts with children in the library must be careful to avoid the type of query that will tend to predispose the child to answer in the way he thinks the questioner wants him to. One may quite easily, though inadvertently, reveal personal feelings and prior knowledge in the wording of a question that will place the child in the position of anticipating what is in the questioner's mind and then formulating an answer he thinks he wants to hear. Allowing the child to come to his own conclusions and to make his own value judgments is important to the development of his maturity as a reader. Miss Veatch illustrates the point in this way:

1. "The Little Red Hen worked hard, didn't she?"
2. "How do you feel about the Little Red Hen?"
In the first question the pupil has little choice but to agree that Little Red Hen did work hard. This is an example of a leading question. On the contrary, the second question allows a pupil to have an opinion of his own and to express it. He is not led into an answer.[61]

Once the child has furnished some background information on what he has derived from the material he has read, a discussion usually follows. During this phase, characters of the book or story are evaluated, various incidents that are basic to the plot or that may have especially interested the youngster are analyzed, comparisons with other stories may be made, and comprehension is checked with some detailed questions which may require the child to skim back into the material to locate specific references. The child may also be asked whether the book was difficult or easy for him to read, what words he got stuck on or didn't know, and what methods he used to attack unknown words encountered. Checklists, which will be discussed in the next chapter, may be used by the teacher at this time to keep a record of the child's progress and mastery of various reading skills.

Oral reading plays an important role during most conferences; it enables the teacher to observe specific difficulties of phrasing that may affect the child's ability to comprehend the material he is reading. It is extremely important that children never be asked to read orally at this time material they have not previously read silently. Oral reading may also reveal to the teacher that the child needs help with certain word analysis skills; he may have difficulty with initial or final consonant sounds, syllabication, or visual clues to vowel sounds. Many children in the middle grades can benefit from additional practice in these areas if instructional sessions are kept brief and the tasks involved don't become a drudgery. Valuable as oral reading is as an adjunct of the reading conference, it need not be a part of every conference. The very capable reader can better use his time during the conference in a more penetrating discussion of his reading experiences or to discuss plans for related creative and sharing activities.

The apportionment of time for reading conferences must be kept relatively flexible. The average conference lasts for about ten minutes but some are much shorter in duration while others require a longer time. The frequency with which teachers see individual children is partly determined by class size. Teachers who have reported on their individualized reading programs often mention that they find they must see some children much more frequently than others. Some children at certain times in the course of the school year may need to see the teacher every day; for other children, one conference a week may suffice. Recommended procedures for managing the scheduling of conferences, as they have been reported in the literature, fall into three basic patterns:

1. Establish a cycle of conferences in which every child in the class is scheduled in turn, though some will require more time than others during the course of their conferences.

2. After getting acquainted with the abilities and needs of the class, establish a ratio system in which certain children are seen once, others twice, etc., in a given cycle. Thus, for instance,

Jim is seen twice for every time that Joan is seen once. Following such a system, it is necessary to periodically modify or adjust the ratios as individual needs change during the year.

3. The scheduling of conferences should be almost entirely on a voluntary basis, that is children are invited at the beginning of the reading period to sign their names on the blackboard if they wish to see the teacher that day. Proponents of this system assume, though, that it may be necessary for the teacher to add names of certain children he feels he needs to see on a particular day.

Regardless of what patterns or procedures are followed in the scheduling and conduct of the reading conference, it is extremely important that the discussion be a friendly and relaxed one and that it be permitted, if there is indication that needs or opportunities exist, to wander as far afield of reading as necessary. Beyond the sphere of reading guidance and instruction, these conferences may at times offer valuable entries into possibilities for ameliorating emotional or social difficulties, certainly not in the deliberate way that a psychologist might, but in the incidental and sensitive man-to-child sort of way that can contribute a measure of therapeutic value. Regarding this and related benefits of the opportunity for personal contact that is afforded by these conferences, Walter Barbe has commented:

The teacher is in a decidedly better position to come to know the student better individually, and to talk over with him any problems he may want to discuss with her. This added time with the children individually should put the teacher in a better position to know to refer particular children for any special attention. . . .

The individual conference period may well be a remedial period for some children. The child who is far below the class level in reading . . . is better able to find satisfaction in reading at his own level without the embarrassment of having to stumble along in material that is too difficult in front of his fellow classmates.

The individual conference is essentially a counseling session. The classroom teacher who has no formal training in counseling, as such, would do well to examine some of the literature on counseling techniques, as well as spend some time in in-service training developing this particular skill. So much depends on the teacher's effective use of the short period of time which she has with the child that preplanning is absolutely essential.[62]

TEACHER AND PUPIL RECORD KEEPING

There seems to be general agreement among those who have written about individualized reading that (1) records kept by both the children and the teacher are an essential adjunct to the program and can yield a multiplicity of useful purposes, and (2) the keynote in designing and maintaining these records should be simplicity. By the time that children reach the middle grades they are able to assume a considerable responsibility for keeping accurate records of their reading activities and they appear to be eager to do so, for pre-teen-agers delight in accumulating almost anything if a given quantity shows promise of increasing; moreover, children of this age group seem to need some concrete evidences of where they have been, what they have accomplished, and where they are going. This is not to say that record keeping necessarily comes naturally to children, for it usually requires considerable instruction and guidance on the part of the teacher, especially during the early stages of the program, and periodic checks and follow-throughs as the program progresses. Realizing the importance of their records, children readily understand the need for keeping them accurate and legible.

The most important records that children are ordinarily responsible for in the individualized reading program are chronologically arranged bibliographies of the books that they read during the school year. Entries are made on these records at the time the book is chosen and when the book is completed. Some writers suggest that these records be kept on loose leaf paper or large cards which are divided into columns with appropriate headings (date, author, title, publisher, pages). Some prefer the use of an open-ended bibliographic form because of the variance in the length of titles and authors' names, as well as in the sizes of children's handwriting. The children

keep records on a 5x8 card and these are filed
alphabetically according to the children's last
names in a box which is kept near the book collection. When a card is completed it is filed in a separate section and a new one is started. Thus one
fifth-grader's second card looked like *Example A*.

Example A.
> KEITH, TED   II
>> (6) 10/11—*Lost Statesmen*, by Edwin P. Hoyt.
>>   Chicago: Reilly and Lee. Pages 3-224.
>> (7) 10/15—*What Then, Roman?* by Shirley Arora.
>>   Chicago: Follett. Pages 5-176.
>> (8) 10/21—*Boats and Ships from A to Z*, by Anne Alexander.
>>   Chicago: Rand McNally. Pages 1-64.
>> (9) 10/25—*Great Ghost Stories*, edited by Herbert van Thal.
>>   New York: Hill and Wang. Pages 3-182.
>> (10) 10/31—*Book of Small Boat Sailing*, by Bill Cox.
>>   Philadelphia: Lippincott. Pages 3-96.

Such running accounts of a child's reading provides him with a source of personal satisfaction
in his accomplishments, allows him, his teachers
and the librarian to periodically evaluate his development, and provides a valuable record to aid
all three in planning for future reading experiences.

Another particularly useful type of record to
which children can make valuable contributions
is a file of reviews and reactions to books which
are contained in the school or classroom library.
Such records may also be kept on 5x8 cards and
filed according to the last name of the author

of the book. When a child completes a book he may prepare a card (see *Example B*) which may later be consulted by children who are considering the same book as their next choice.

Example B.

FREUCHEN, PETER

Whaling Boy

This exciting book tells about a ten-year-old Danish boy who goes to work as a mess boy on the whaling ship of the best sea captain in Denmark of about a hundred years ago. If it was as long as *Moby Dick*, I would have liked it better.

PATRICK FARRELL   9/30/62

Children can be encouraged to make the kind of comments about books that will help others decide whether they would like to read the same title. They may briefly describe the plot, tell some piece of information they learned as a result of reading the book, describe one of the book's characters that interested them most, or anything else that they consider might help someone else decide about taking the book.

Simplicity is as important for the teacher's record system as it is for the children's; if record keeping becomes too cumbersome or complicated, the teacher will find himself bogged down with clerical detail. Several writers have suggested that the teacher's records of children's progress be kept in a loose-leaf note book, one page for each child. When a conference is held with an individual youngster, the date of the conference, the title of the material that he is reading, special difficulties that he may be encountering, his reactions to the content of the reading material, and other comments the teacher may feel are important are recorded. Such a running record reveals over a period of time a great deal of useful information about each child's progress and growth in reading power. Such records also provide a useful reference for the determination of what special help groups may be needed and what specific children should be included in these groups. Then too, such records help bridge the lapse in time between each of the conferences that are held with individual children. They are also useful as part of the total information and knowledge that the teacher draws upon during the periodic evaluations for parent conferences and report cards. Teachers and librarians find it helpful to have these records before them when they are discussing plans for coordinated efforts in the reading program.

IMPLICATIONS FOR THE LIBRARIAN

It is probable that one major factor that will help determine a teacher's feeling of confidence and experiences of success in the individualized reading program is his prior knowledge of the books that children are reading. If there is a limitation to the potential of this method of reading instruction, it lies in the degree of knowledge that the teacher has about children's literature in general and the books his children are reading in particular. Obviously, if the teacher is familiar with the book he is discussing with a child during a reading conference, he will more effectively be able to guide the child in his selection of main ideas or in his analysis of story characters or plot situations. While the teacher may use his lack of familiarity with a certain book to motivate a child to tell him about it purposefully, he is at a distinct advantage if he knows the book and consequently is able to direct the discussion on the basis of that knowledge. The librarian is, of course, the key person in communicating to teachers about the world of children's books and in interpreting the library's collection for them. The more individualized the reading program is, in the school in which he serves, the more vitally necessary the function of teacher advisement becomes for the school librarian. There are several approaches that might be used to achieve this aim, among which are:

1. Provision for regular and continuous in-service education for teachers in the field of children's literature. While attendance by teachers must be entirely voluntary, the need for this type of program is very great since teacher training institutions do not ordinarily at the present

time adequately prepare their students in this area.

2. Provisions for periodic book talks to teachers about new arrivals in the library or covering groups of books in the collection about specific subjects or related to the curriculum or interest of specific grade levels. The latter course may be the preferable one, since the subjects of the book talks may be announced in advance, so that only teachers who are concerned or interested in the area need attend.

3. Development of clerical methods to keep teachers informed about the content of new additions to the library's collection. One way of doing this might be to prepare brief annotations for individual volumes, as they are added, on ditto or mimeographed stencils which are ruled off in such a way that the printed sheets may be cut into 3x5 slips. These could then be collated into packets and routed to the teachers. The teachers might then file these slips for future reference during reading guidance or reading conferences. In time, each teacher would have a useful key to the library's collection.

4. It was suggested earlier that children can prepare very useful annotations on the books that they have read. In some situations it may be useful for the librarian to supervise this activity as part of a book club's responsibility. Book

clubs, with this and other duties, under the librarian's guidance can be both a needed source of enrichment for the members and an extremely effective method of communication between the librarian and the classroom.

Many of the ingredients of the reading conference between the teacher and the child can be carried over into the library, though in a less formal structure, as the librarian discussess children's reading experiences with them. Many who have reported on their individualized reading programs in the literature have commented that one major difference between ability-grouped basal reading and individualized reading that they have observed is that in the latter type of program children seem always to be talking about the books they are reading or have recently completed, not just during the reading period, but in odd moments throughout the day. Discerning librarians are apt to find a great many opportunities during each day to keep in touch with children's progress in reading and to offer what guidance may seem to be appropriate. Additionally, these informal chats can help the librarian stay abreast of the continuously shifting pattern of interests among the children, which, if reflected in a dynamic and evolving book collection can give great impetus to the momentum of the entire reading program.

Records like the ones which have been described can be of great value to the librarian in many phases of his work with children and teachers. The child's cumulative bibliography of his reading over an extended period of time should, for instance, help to make reading guidance in the library more meaningful. To enter into effective partnership in the instructional team in reading, librarians need to know as much as possible about each of the children they serve. Librarians may find it helpful to keep on file a card for each child on which data pertinent to book selection and reading guidance can be recorded. Among the items that might be entered for each child are:

1. The name, age, and grade of the child.

2. Scores received on reading achievement tests and the intelligence quotient.

3. A list or description of the child's areas of interest.

4. Some data related to the child's past reading experiences, such as a list of titles that he has especially enjoyed.

5. Those areas, particularly in reference to reading skills, where the child needs special help or additional assistance.

If the children's source of reading materials is primarily the library rather than a classroom book collection, the cards carrying reviews of books, which are described on page 93 might be kept on file in the library.

VI. RELATED LEARNING AND
CREATIVE ACTIVITIES

READING SKILLS INSTRUCTION

Information which is gathered during reading conferences or noted informally by the teacher and the librarian indicates the kinds of short-term instructional groups which need to be established from time to time and the children who should be included in each of the groups. Such groups, according to Jeannette Veatch, must be organized on the basis of one specific purpose that will not change while the group is in existence.[63]

In a basal reading type of program, the fourth-, fifth-, and sixth-grade curriculum is largely devoted to the reteaching and refinement of skills which are first taught in the primary grades. In theory, the child who has completed the third-grade reading program has achieved relative independence in word attack skills and simply needs reviewing, reteaching, and a good deal of experience in reading varied materials to strengthen these skills to the point where reading becomes effortless. The theory, of course, is not always translated into reality, and children do enter the fourth-grade who have not mastered the basic fundamentals of the reading process. The problem for middle-grade teachers is that children vary greatly in the specifics of their reading deficiencies. In basal reading instruction, as the child progresses through a book of appropriate difficulty, he often is exposed to accompanying basic instruction in skills that he has mastered whereas those areas in which he really needs considerable help may be neglected. Unlike a subject such as arithmetic, reading involves an extremely complicated interplay of a multiplicity of skills which are required for successful mastery. The flexibility of the individualized method of reading instruction offers the teacher and the librarian the opportunity to approach and deal with children as individuals rather than as groups.

One indispensable tool that may be used by members of the instructional team in reading to keep an accurate check on the status of each child's mastery of the reading process is the skills checklist. Several excellent types of checklists have been developed specifically for use in individualized reading. The use of these detailed records or profiles of individual strengths and weaknesses meets what has been the major objection of critics of individualized reading: that this method of instruction ignores the development of reading skills. One most thorough and complete set of checklists has been developed by

Walter Barbe for each of the six grade levels of instruction in the elementary school.[64] His lists for the middle grades are each divided into four major sections: Vocabulary, Word Attack Skills, Comprehension, and Oral Reading. A separate list is kept for each child and appropriate notations are made on it throughout the year as the child masters each of the skills involved. Some of these skills relate directly to the role of the librarian in the instructional program. The section quoted below is Part III (Comprehension) on the fifth-grade list; it illustrates how closely instruction in library skills ties into this key area of reading ability:

III. Comprehension
A. Locating information
  1. Table of contents.
    a. Examine tables of contents of several books.
    b. List titles and have pupils use table of contents to locate pages.
  2. Examine books to find: title page, picture, key, guide words, publisher, copyright year.
B. Reference materials
  1. The encyclopedia.
    a. Topics arranged alphabetically.
    b. Show meaning of characters on back of each volume.
    c. Compare dictionaries and encyclopedias for differences of materials.
    d. Pupils should know names of important children's encyclopedias.
  2. The atlas and maps.
    a. Examine atlas to find answers for questions on location, relative size, direction and distance.
    b. Use maps to explain latitude and longitude. Compare with known facts about streets and highways.

3. Magazines and newspapers. Use to supply more recent information than textbook could contain.
4. Proper use of dictionary.
5. Time tables.
   a. Reading and interpreting.
   b. Following directions.
6. Card catalogue.
   a. Explain that every book has its place on the shelf.
   b. Each class of books has its own call number.
   c. Examine cards: author, title, subject.
   d. Give practice in location of titles and call numbers.
7. Using a telephone book.
8. Catalogues.

The remaining list of skills under this section dealing with the area of comprehension for the fifth-grade level might appropriately be developed jointly by the teacher and the librarian:

C. Reading to organize
   1. Outlining. Use roman numerals and letters.
   2. Establish a sequence. Pupils list sentences in order of event.
   3. Follow directions.
   4. Summarize.
D. Note taking
   1. From reading.
   2. From lectures.
E. Reading for information
   1. To derive pleasure.
   2. To form sensory impressions.
   3. To develop imagery.
   4. To understand characters.
      a. Physical appearance.
      b. Emotional make-up.[65]

Librarians serving schools that have adopted the individualized method of reading instruction will be interested in familiarizing themselves with the techniques that teachers use to promote growth in each of the four major areas—Vocabulary, Word Analysis, Comprehension, and Oral Reading—of the reading program.

Teachers who have contributed to the literature on individualized reading reveal that they use various combinations of four basic approaches to develop children's reading vocabularies:

1. During the reading-to-the-teacher phase of the reading conference, the teacher is able to tell the child the words he does not know. This method is functionally effective because the child recognizes the need to know these words so that he can understand the story fully, and his time isn't wasted, as it may be in the basal program, with presentations of words that he may already know.

2. Some teachers prefer to spend a part of their time during the reading period walking around the classroom while the children are reading silently. When a child meets a word he doesn't know, he is encouraged to signal the teacher, who then moves over to discuss it with him.

3. Children are sometimes paired off in teams during the reading period so that they can help each other. Some teachers report that they pair off children so that a strong reader has a less capable reader as his partner; others base such

pairs on the free sociometric choices of the children.

4. Children are encouraged to keep a written record of words that present difficulty as they progress with their books. Time is then provided in the schedule when they may use their dictionaries to explore pronunciations and meanings, or they may share the words they have found with the group for all-class discussions.

Instruction to develop word attack skills is ordinarily handled in the small special-purpose groups that are established from time to time by the teacher as a result of his observations of common needs. The following is a listing of some of the purposes for which these groups might be formed:

1. To identify initial consonants or consonant blends in known words and apply to unknown words.

2. To identify medial or final consonants and consonant blends in known words and apply to unknown words.

3. To identify vowel sounds as they occur in consistent patterns (bite, mite; meal, seal; bit, sit; bar, far; etc.).

4. To identify and analyze compound words (bookcase, sunburn, platform, etc.).

5. To identify and analyze the function of prefixes, suffixes, and endings in known words and apply to unknown words.

6. To identify systems for forming plurals and verb tenses.

7. To note root words and their derived and inflected forms (turn, turning, turned, return, turns, etc.).

8. To develop the generalizations about patterns of syllabication through an analysis of known words and then apply them to unknown words.

9. To learn to use context as an aid in the identification of unknown words.

10. To learn to use the rules of alphabetizing, develop speed in their application, and apply to the location of entries in the dictionary.

11. To develop an understanding of how symbols are used in pronunciation respellings and how correct pronunciations may be verified through the use of the dictionary.

12. To use the dictionary to find antonyms, synonyms, and homonyms.[66]

The types of probing and purposeful discussions that take place during the individual reading conferences make important contributions to the development of children's ability to comprehend the material they read. In addition, teachers report using textbooks in literature, science, and social studies for experiences that are designed to improve comprehension abilities. Paul McKee has cited four basic purposes for which children in the middle grades should have guided experiences in reading:

1. Reading to get the general import.—The pupil must do much reading with the simple purpose of getting the general import of the selection at hand. . . . As a rule the reading is to be done rapidly with a recreatory rather than a work attitude. No critical weighing of particular elements is required, and brief parts of the material may be skipped without doing harm to the realization of the purpose.

2. Reading to get details.—Sometimes a pupil must read a selection or a part of a selection for the purpose of getting all the details it presents on a given topic or question. . . . Such reading is to be done with relatively slow speed, with a specific topic or question in mind, and usually with a work attitude. . .

3. Reading to generalize.—Frequently the reader must read . . . in order to build up a generalization or a conclusion. . . . Such reading can be done with moderate speed, although the reader must relate correctly the elements presented, think of implications of statements, weigh elements against one another, and combine the proper elements to make the generalization.

4. Read to analyze critically.—At times the reader must read critically with the purpose of judging the worthwhileness of a selection or a part of a selection. He may need to decide whether a given story is suitable for dramatization or whether it would be improved by the use of a different ending. He may need to decide whether a given factual selection is truthful.[67]

The most important rule regarding the development of oral reading skills is that children should *never* read aloud material they have not first read silently. If there is a second rule that approaches this one in importance it is that there must be strong motives developed for reading aloud if growth in oral interpretation is to be effectively promoted. As children move into the middle grades an increasing amount of the reading that they do is silent, but there is still need for attention to the development of oral reading skills, if only because of their functional use in everyday life. Lillian Gray and Dora Reese have cited a few of the situations in which children may later use the skills of oral interpretation:

1. Provide enjoyment in a social group.
2. Answer specific questions.
3. Substantiate answers challenged by others in a group.
4. Share content to which all do not have access.
5. Give directions for others to follow.
6. Make a report to a group.
7. Present announcements or other information to a group.
8. Present questions, problems, riddles for a group to answer or solve.
9. Prepare for a dramatization.
10. Test fluency and accuracy.[68]

In addition to the individual guidance and instruction in oral reading techniques that is given to children during the reading conference, skills in this area are developed or strengthened by oral reading activities in which the whole or a part of the class participates, storytelling by the teacher, the librarian, or by the children themselves, work with dramatizations, and a great deal of listening by the children to oral interpretation of a high quality. The skills of oral reading are not entirely separate from those of silent reading, and improvement in oral interpretation and delivery often follows improvement in word attack and comprehension skills, as the child, for instance, develops the ability to read in idea units rather than in word units. Provision for oral reading experiences also gives teachers and librarians additional opportunites to stress the understanding that speed of reading must be adjusted to the purpose for which reading is being done as well as the type of material being read.

RELATED CREATIVE ACTIVITIES

There is ample evidence in the reports that teachers have written describing their individualized reading programs that children's reading experiences may be successfully channeled into a wide variety of related creative activities. The teacher and the librarian working together in this type of program play an important role in stimulating and guiding children's reactions to the books that they read into rich and satisfying creative expressions. Children's books are a natural springboard into culminating creative activities, as Nancy Larrick has pointed out:

Fairy tales, legends, and tall tales suggest more storytelling by the children themselves. Or they invite retelling by the children through dramatization, puppetry or pantomime. Pleasure in poetry prompts many children to write their own poems.

The plays they put on and the stories they write may be simple, even crude, if judged by adult standards. Their poetry may lack both rhyme and rhythm. But the children who have produced them are moving ahead because of new confidence in their ability to communicate.

A child's literary and artistic creations are significant for the effect they have on his attitude and behavior. The purpose is not to develop a Shakespeare in every fourth grade but rather to give each child the opportunity to test the wings of his imagination.[69]

The question of book reports is a thorny one with no easy answer. Proponents of individualized reading unanimously agree that written reports should not be required either every time a book is completed or in stipulated quantities each month or semester. Such a requirement would interfere with the basic philosophy of the program, the motivational factors that guide the reader, and the genuineness of the seeking and self-selective process.[70] On the other hand, children in the middle grades, as Fern Shipley has pointed out, enjoy recording their reactions to their reading experiences in a written form, provided the activity is kept simple, flexible, and largely voluntary.[71]

I have encouraged the children I work with to react in written form only to those books about which they feel they have something they want to say or some reaction they want to crystallize verbally—whether it be positive or negative in nature—and that in doing so they consider alternatives to the traditional recounting of the plot. As a guide, a list of possible questions to be answered was developed cooperatively by the class:

1. What was the setting of the story? Where was the action laid?

2. What was the time or period setting of the story or book?

3. What were some of the personality contrasts which existed between or among various characters in the book?

4. What feelings did the story arouse in you—anger, excitement, fear?

5. If you were one of the characters in the story would you have done what he did?

6. What was the plot structure like? Did it build up to a climax, or was the action sustained throughout? Was the story told in flashback form?

7. What was your reaction to the hero—admiration, scorn, distaste, hatred, satisfaction?

8. Which one of the characters in the story did you identify with or admire most? Which one did you like least? Why?

9. What did you learn from the book that you didn't know before?

10. Has the book suggested other kinds of things that you'd like to look for to read?

A most extensive listing of follow-up activities expressly designed for individualized reading to appear to date was developed by Maida Sharpe, who used the various activities successfully in the course of her work with elementary school children:

I. Fictional Stories

1. Recording
   a. Keep individual records of titles read; dates; pages.
   b. "Beginning book report": Title, author, publisher. List important characters: illustrate, name. For more capable learner: comment about the book—what liked or not liked; why someone else should read it.
   c. If book contains several stories, list titles of most interesting ones, as well as book title.
2. Illustrating
   a. Illustrate main characters.
   b. Pictures of main events in sequence.
   c. Illustrate most exciting events, or best liked.
   d. Make book jacket for story.
   e. Make diorama of favorite part of story.
   f. Make miniature stage setting for exciting scene.
3. Committee work
   a. Prepare a dramatization of part of the story.
   b. Prepare parts to identify characters in story.
   c. Make list of questions to ask others who have read story.
   d. Prepare answers to such questions.
   e. Report on books or stories relating to unit studies sections of basal readers.
   f. Arrange book displays: "Our Favorite Books"; new and old books.
   g. Classify book lists according to subjects; illustrate.
4. Oral reporting—audience situations.
   a. Show illustration and tell about it.
   b. Prepare interesting part of story to read; tell why liked.
   c. Decide if story could be true; could not be. Choose selections from story to read orally to prove decision.
   d. Interview adults concerning author; report orally.

e. Tell portion of a story: predict how it might end, or make up different ending, or tell how reader would end it and why, if he were the author.

5. Written activities

a. Write title or sentence for illustrations.

b. Write sentence which tells of author's illustrations.

c. Make list of unusual, or difficult words.

d. Write something about the author (upper grades).

e. Write answers to blackboard or mimeographed questions prepared by teacher; group; committee.

f. Creative writing: original poems, plays, stories, essays; illustrate.

g. Select important news and write a summary for class or school newspaper.

h. Make bibliography: organize for mutual interests.

II. Factual Interests

1. Recording

a. Make a record of what was done to follow directions of simple experiment.

b. Keep records of temperatures, weights, measures.

c. Title and pages where directions were found.

2. Research

a. To identify collections such as shells, stamps.

b. Make scrapbooks of pictures of collections—pets, animals social studies, interests, science.

c. Find picture words to illustrate each letter of alphabet: find pictures to illustrate words or draw own.

d. Find stories which will answer questions of the group concerning social studies, science, other interests.

e. Before taking a trip: plan what to see, how to go, places of interest to visit.

3. Committee work

a. Groups work to find facts concerning interests.

b. Organize and record information.

c. Organize bulletin board, book table, or collections.

d. Classify book lists according to subjects.

e. Illustrating: time lines, murals, experiments.

f. Compile bibliography for background of current news events; arrange display.

4. Oral reporting—make preparation for the following:

a. Tell about a simple experiment and results.

    b. Report findings concerning group interests which have been learned through trips or interviews.
    c. Tell about collections.
    d. Report interesting facts found when reading about interests.
5. Written activities
    a. Make lists of subject words: colors, food, phases of science, flowers, pets, etc.
    b. Make a picture dictionary illustrating picture or subject words.
    c. Find answers to questions of the group; list pages; make a bibliography file for reference.
    d. Record references to information found in library: pictures; junior encyclopedias, topical interests; include topic, pages, authorities, dates.
    e. Summarize information learned from charts, graphs, maps,
    f. Compile bibliography of mutual interest; make 3x5 card file for reference and expansions.[72]

Activities such as these can make tremendous contributions to the reading program's objective of making reading a great deal more than simply one of the subjects that occupies part of the school day. They carry reading into every area of the elementary school curriculum and hopefully move children toward the two major goals of individualized reading instruction: the mastery of the reading process to the point where the act of reading becomes effortless, and the creation of permanent interest and participation in reading and the rewards reading has to offer.

IMPLICATIONS FOR LIBRARIANS

School librarians have, of course, traditionally assumed an instructional role in training children how to use the resources of the library. The purpose of the first section of the present chapter has been to indicate how closely these instructional activities are related to the reading curriculum in the middle grades of the elementary school. The librarian can and does make important contributions to the child's growth in many of the basic reading skills. Two areas wherein the coordinated efforts of the teacher and the librarian are particularly important in this respect are the teaching of the dictionary and the glossary— the most sophisticated of the various word analysis skills, according to William Gray[73]—and the teaching of the methods of locating and recording information, a phase of the comprehension skills. Briefly outlined, these two skill areas ordinarily embrace the following sequence of content:

I. Training in the use of the dictionary and glossary.
1. Location skills.
   a. Knowledge of alphabetical sequence.
   b. Ability to use guide words.
   c. Division of the dictionary into thirds and fourths.
2. Pronunciation skills.
   a. Recognition of vowel and consonant phonemes and association with their respective symbols.
   b. Use of pronunciation key to identify consonant and vowel sounds.
   c. Recognition of the function of visual syllabic divisions and accent marks.
   d. Ability to blend syllables into whole words.
3. Meaning skills.
   a. Comprehension of the definitions of meaning given in the dictionary

b. Ability to determine which definition explains the meaning that the author had in mind when he used the word.

c. Ability to tune a definition back into context in which the unknown word was encountered, i.e., add "-ing" to the definition of suspend for suspending.

II. Locating Information and Recording It.[74]

1. Parts of a book.

a. Table of contents.

b. Index.

c. Other parts (title page, pictures, maps and charts, publisher, copyright year, etc.).

2. Reference materials in reading.

a. Maps, graphs, and tables.

b. Encyclopedias.

c. Specialized reference books—biographical, quotation, geographic, literary, historical.

d. Yearbooks.

3. Library skills

a. Arrangement and use of the card catalog.

b. Book classifications.

4. Vertical file and periodicals.

a. Type, arrangement, and value of vertical file collection.

b. Magazines as a supplement to the book collection, types and purposes, periodical indexes and how to interpret.

5. Bibliography and note-taking.

a. Definition, form, and examples of bibliographies.

b. Places to look for references for a bibliography.

c. The process of note-taking—skimming, careful reading of selected parts, rereading to take numbered notes.

Librarians can do a great deal to foster the improvement of oral reading skills. They have traditionally taken a lead in developing standards for oral reading during the periods that they reserve for reading aloud to groups that visit the library in order to stimulate reading interests, share appreciations, or simply entertain. Beyond these immediate goals, a regular program of reading aloud to children can be used to demonstrate to them the many techniques which the skilled oral reader employs to project sensory imagery, moods, and emotional tones to the listeners. Children sometimes have difficulty interpreting material orally because they are timid about the prospect of emotionalizing before a group. As the librarian projects his own and the author's feelings during these sessions of reading aloud, he may well reassure the inhibited youngster who tends to read in a repressed monotone that dramatic reading isn't really foolish. Certainly, good examples of oral interpretation are much more effective than analytical criticism in promoting these skills among young people.

Maida Sharpe's comprehensive listing of creative follow-up activities (pages 112-14) suggests several areas where the librarian may lend direct support to the teacher in promoting these invaluable experiences. Christine Gilbert has pointed out that the attitude of the librarian and the atmosphere of the library can have an important influence in stimulating children not only to read tastefully and widely but also creatively. She has made a number of practical suggestions that librarians may follow to foster the creative aspects of the individualized reading program. Among these are:

1. Informal Dramatization of Stories: Frequently after telling or reading a story, children enjoy acting it out. This is done informally without props or scenery. Each child takes a different part, even to being inanimate objects such as rocks or trees!

2. Illustrating a Story: At times the librarian may read a story without showing the illustrations and suggest that some of the children might like to make original illustrations for the story. In most instances children will choose different episodes to illustrate, giving him an opportunity to see the various qualities in the story which appeal to different children.

3. Book Discussions: The librarian can often have a lively book discussion by telling something about his favorite books and having children do the same. This is a painless way of reporting and gives the librarian an opportunity to help students learn to analyze the qualities in books which make them appealing.

4. Puppet Plays: Often favorite stories may be simply and easily made into puppet plays. The shy child finds this a particularly good way to share his interests in books for the puppet can express his feelings for him.

5. Book Marks: By having children design book marks for their library books many interesting results may be obtained. Sometimes the book marks carry information on the care of books and at other times they are related to book characters or suggest other good books to read.

6. Book Figurines: Little figures of favorite book characters can be carved from wood or soap or made of clay, paper or other material. They may costume a doll in the dress of their favorite character or make a knight in armor or a replica of their beloved horse.[75]

The author also suggests that the librarian include children in the process of book selection, the many creative activities that can be correlated to the observance of book week, the develment of book displays and exhibits, and book reviewing for school and town newspapers. "The

librarian one remembers," concludes Miss Gilbert, "is the one who loves books and by his skill
in opening up the world of books helps others to
love them too."

VII. EVALUATING THE PROGRAM

WHAT THE TEACHERS SAY

"When Dave entered my sixth-grade room, in September," writes Ann Noel,[76] "I was told that he had trouble with reading. Reading test scores reflected his inability to read." So begins a story typical of the many empirical reports written by teachers testifying to the visible and dramatic success that they experienced with techniques of individualized reading instruction. Often these stories concern children for whom the world of reading suddenly opened up because the opportunity to learn to read at their own levels and at their own pace remained open to them and, as Alice Miel has commented, the opportunity did not come as, 'forced feeding' nor was it accompanied with 'doses of shame'." [77] Miss Noel continues:

Mental tests identified him as a dull-normal child. He had already put in an extra year's time in the fifth-grade. Records from his first three years at school presented the picture of an exceedingly shy, immature child inclined to sit passively and demonstrate little initiative in making contact with classmates and teacher . . .

Roaming far afield in the neighborhood after school hours, he felt the world around him alive and vivid. He was keenly observant of people and things and incidents, even though he had no facility in reading to help him clarify his thinking or to help him place his findings in their proper perspective.

Miss Noel's description could easily fit a great number of children who fail in reading under a basal type of program; they may or may not be below average intellectually, but for some combination of reasons — physical, mental, emotional—they are not ready to learn to read when most of the other children in their class are. As a result, they, falling further and further behind find themselves consistently placed in the lowest reading group and gradually developing a strong distaste for reading. By the time some combination of operative factors suddenly makes them ready to read, they have developed such a strong block against it, or indeed toward everything to do with school, that they remain permanently debilitated.

Feeling that David's growth in reading would be significant only if it enabled him to enrich his experiences and grow personally and socially, Miss Noel made every effort to get close to the boy by fostering a close personal relationship. Later she encouraged him to explore quantities of books so that he could seek out what would be challenging and provocative material for him. This he did, and even in the early days of his individualized sessions with Miss Noel materials which he could not then read caught his imagination. "This is a book that I can hardly wait to read," he said of *Robin Hood*.

At the end of the school year, test scores revealed that David had made more than three years' growth in reading. He had begun the year as a non-reader. He finished an enthusiastic reader . . . He went home the last day of school with his arms filled with some favorite books which he had spotted but had not had time to read.

What was wrong with Dave? Had the primary teachers failed? Was he a remedial case? I am not certain that anything was *wrong*. I suspect that Dave learned to read by the process most natural, most economical, most effective for him. In terms of his own unique potential for growth, it may be that he made normal progress. . . . He is a child who touches life in a great variety of ways and seizes information therefrom. He has now developed reading skills to the point where he may thoughtfully, unhurriedly read from a number of sources to straighten out confusion and falsehood.[78]

Teachers, administrators, and supervisors who have contributed to the literature on individualized reading often report the results of reading achievement tests to establish the validity of the method in promoting growth in children's reading power, but they uniformly reject such test results as the sole method of evaluation. Alvina Burrows reflects this philosophy regarding the evaluation of reading by citing some of the limitations of the standardized reading tests and offering some supplementary criteria that teachers and librarians may employ when they evaluate children's growth in this area:

Helpful as test are for general purposes and, in conjunction with other data, for individual diagnosis, they do not tell us enough. They do not tell us whether a child wants to read, whether he has a feeling of responsibility for accurately sharing his findings. Tests do not tell us whether a child reads widely,

whether he is developing taste and descrimination in reading,
whether his reading opens new possibilities for exploration.
Yet without these attributes a child, even though he rates successfully on a reading test, has nonetheless missed the essence
of reading. To assure their development is what a reading program is for!

These elements are largely subjective in type; but they can
be noted by observant teachers and parents. At least five kinds
of reaction need to be considered in order to evaluate them in
the middle grades:

1. Does a child choose to read or does he elude reading?
2. Does he find reading material related to his interests?
3. Does he feel responsibility for reporting factual material
accurately?
4. Does he try increasingly to try to help himself in reading?
5. Is he beginning to vary his reading techniques according
to the nature of the content and his purposes?[79]

CHILDREN'S REACTION TO THE PROGRAM

Several teachers report in the literature of having asked their classes to comment orally or in
writing on their feelings about individualized
reading. Usually these are classes that have had
a basal reading program with ability grouping
during the year prior to the one being reported
on. Margaret Largent asked such a group to
write about their reactions at the end of third
grade and then divided the responses for analysis
according to each child's general ability as a
reader. She reports that:

The good readers said:
"I like reading this year because I don't have to read the
same word over and over."
"I can read as fast as I like and don't have to wait for the
slow ones. Sometimes we couldn't finish the story in a group."

Average readers made comments like these:

"I didn't like the old stories; I could hear the other groups reading them, so they were not new. Now I can read any kind of story."

"It's more fun because I can read all the science books I like. I couldn't read long enough in a group."

Slower readers said:

"I can read the books I like without being teased about 'baby books'."

"I don't like to read in a group; if I make a mistake, the others laugh. I like to read to you alone."[80]

Phyllis Parkin, a fourth-grade teacher, recorded the comments of her children several months after they made a transition from a basal to an individualized reading program. Among the remarks made by the youngsters were:

"I like this kind of reading because I can read as fast as I want to."

"Last year everyone knew I was in the second group until I got good enough to move into the highest one. This year no one knows what group I'm in because there aren't any groups."

"I like individualized reading because I don't have to wait for anyone to finish a story before I can go on to a new one."

"This kind of reading is more fun because I can find out what I want to for myself. I don't have to answer questions that someone else makes up."

"I like individual reading because the teacher doesn't pass out books and say, 'Today we're going to begin to read this together.'"

"The reason I'd rather have individual reading is because I can ask a friend to read with me or I can read alone if I rather.

"I like to read about all the books the others are reading." That helps me to choose my next book sometimes."

"In this kind of reading the teacher just helps those who need help. The rest of us don't have to learn over again what we already know."[81]

In her observations of the children, Miss Parkin noted, "freedom of choice and that joy that accompanies it . . . release from the stigma of the group label . . . a change of emphasis from competition with the group to competition with one's self."

EXPERIMENTAL STUDIES

An increasing number of controlled experimental studies are being conducted by individual school systems to determine the relative merits of individualized reading instruction when compared to ability-grouped basal reading instruction. Approximately twelve of these studies have been reported in descriptive detail in educational journals since 1954. A much larger number of studies have been completed as unpublished masters' and doctoral projects. These studies are ordinarily designed with an equal number of experimental (individualized reading) and control (basal reading) groups, as evenly matched as possible on the basis of reading ability, intelligence, age, and often socio-economic status. Teachers are frequently assigned to one or the other of the two types of instructional group on the basis of random selection; this is an important control on the variable of teacher attitude.

Commenting on an unpublished doctoral study made by Clare Walker[82] in grades four five, and six, Robert Karlin observed:

One experiment has been completed in Michigan. Two groups of children were matched . . . and taught by student teachers under the supervision of critic teachers. One group followed a basal reader approach, while the other engaged in individualized reading. The data showed no significant difference between the groups in reading gains. The student teachers did report that the children in the individualized group showed greater interest in reading and read more books than the children in the basal reader group.[83]

In January, 1961, Irene Vite reported on her analysis of the major experimental studies appearing in the literature since 1952 on the subject of basal versus individualized reading instruction.[84] Of these seven studies, four showed significant test results favoring individualized reading while three showed results favoring basal reading. One researcher who found negative test-score results for individualized reading still concluded that in other factors—greater numbers of books read by the children, better study habits, more favorable attitude toward books and reading—the findings favored individualized reading.[85]

One recent reported study was conducted by the New York City Board of Education's Bureau of Educational Research. It attempted to determine what differential effect, if any, individualized reading has on the scores children attain on standardized reading tests. The study examined and compared the reading gain measured by these tests of children who were given individualized reading in their fourth- and fifth-grade classes against tests of children who had the standard basal reading program during the same period. At the time the study was made, the children were in the sixth grade. The individualized reading group of 351 subjects obtained a significantly higher mean reading score (six months) than the 6,816 members of the control group.[86]

This study is part of a continuing and larger investigation by the school system of New York City to develop a clearer understanding of the processes of individualized reading instruction and the relative contributions that the method makes to children's growth in reading ability, interest, and taste.[87] The study cited concludes:

It is suggested . . . that the positive differential found for the individualized reading group was due to a cluster of factors. By and large there may have been, in theory and in practice, a greater acceptance of, and attention to, differences among children in the individualized classes, and also a greater recognition in class room procedures of reading and learning-to-read as an active thinking-feeling experience. Even if no significant difference in test results had appeared, an investigation of individualized reading by teachers of fourth and fifth grade pupils would be warranted, on the grounds of the contributions of individualized reading to less tangible aspects of children's behavior.[88]

In summary, the experimental studies which have been reported to date on the relative merits of individualized and basal reading instruction, when viewed collectively, seem to indicate:

1. There is no consistent significant loss in reading achievement as measured on standardized reading tests when basal reading programs are replaced with individualized methods of instruction.

2. Children's attitudes toward books and reading seem more positive in the individualized type of reading program.

3. Children read more in individualized reading programs.

4. The individualized reading program seems to help teachers to perceive the children they work with as individuals rather than as groups or classes.

IMPLICATIONS FOR LIBRARIANS

It has already been pointed out that those librarians who serve schools where individualized reading methods of instruction are practiced need to keep in touch with children's reading achievement scores, that they should keep records of these and other data for each child in the school, and that such information along with other factors developed jointly through teacher-librarian consultation should help determine the planning of day-to-day programs in reading which are designed to meet the immediate and long-range needs of individual children. The discussion in the previous chapter, of the role that school librarian can play in fostering those creative activities of the children grow from their experiences, carries with it indications of ways that children's growth in and attitudes toward reading may be observed and to a degree measured. Certainly there is a very fine line, if one exists at all, that separates the functions that a librarian performs in the areas of reading motivation and guidance from the evaluative function, for both go on simultaneously.

Beatrice Hurley suggests that teachers and librarians, as part of their continuing evaluations of children's growth in and through reading experiences, look for the following characteristics of behavior:

1. Children feel at home with books, magazines, and other reading matter, treating them as friends or family.

2. Children use books for pleasure and to add stature to their expanding intellectual horizons.

3. Children become efficient users of library facilities available in classroom, school, neighborhood, and at home.

4. Children share with others those exhilarating, beautiful prose and poetry passages that are making deep and lasting impressions.

5. Children form the habit of reading reflectively, becoming a partner with author and illustrator.

6. Children become increasingly more sensitive in their choices of books, rejecting the mediocre, accepting only the more deeply satisfying kinds of literature.

7. Children build more securely their own standards of values as they experience the heritage of literature that is theirs.

8. Children demonstrate the personal fulfillment derived through reading by using its riches for fuller living, referring often to worthwhile bits of literature to gain inspiration and perspective.

9. Children covet ownership of significant books, realizing that books offer a direct route to knowledge, that they contain a profound morality and respect universal values of living.

10. Children become ever more catholic in their reading tastes, dipping alternately into biography, adventure, folklore, legends, fantasy, realistic and scientific materials—old and new prose and poetry.

11. Children not only know how to read, they love to read.[89]

Because the evaluation of individualized reading programs cannot be confined to the results obtained on reading achievement tests, librarians need to take a far greater part in the evaluative process than they might in situations in which basal reading instruction is involved. It is in the somewhat intangible factors as those types of behavior described above that the proponents of individualized reading claim the greatest advantage.

Aside from the advantages to and effects upon children that an individualized reading program may have, librarians will be concerned with other evaluative problems. They will need to determine the ways in which the implementation of individualized reading programs in their schools affects the nature of library services that they offer, how it may necessitate revision in budgetary requirements and staff needs, and how it may alter or modify policies of book selection.

The impact of the individualized reading program upon the elementary school library and some of the unsolved problems that will emerge from it will be discussed in the concluding chapter.

VIII. SUMMARY AND CONCLUSIONS

HOW THE LIBRARIAN SUPPORTS THE PROGRAM

One of the two hypotheses involved in the present study maintains that a basic requirement for the successful implementation of the individualized method of teaching reading in the elementary school is the expert assistance of a professionally trained librarian working cooperatively with children and teachers. The main part of the study has been devoted to a description of the philosophy and methodology of individualized reading as a basis for determining the various ways that the school librarian can support and enrich the program.

Among the ways that the librarian works with teachers of individualized reading to support and implement their classroom programs are the following:

1. He works in close partnership with the teachers in all aspects of reading guidance, supporting and supplementing what they are doing as part of their reading programs in the classrooms, so that the "teachable moment" is identified, analyzed, and exploited for each individual child.

2. He keeps teachers informed about the content and range of materials the library has to offer in support of the program, and he does this in such a way that the teacher's knowledge of children's literature in general and the library's collection in particular becomes a resource of growing importance and effectiveness.

3. He helps individual teachers to select and use appropriate books at the right time for the right children.

4. He exchanges information with teachers about children's individual needs, not only regarding library skills but in terms of the total reading skills complex and aspects of social and psychological adjustment that may relate to reading.

5. He assumes direct responsibility for the teaching of those reading skills that may be taught more appropriately and effectively in the library setting than in the classroom.

6. He offers programs of in-service education in children's literature, the use of the library, the resources and services of the library, and the changing nature and scope of the collection as teachers indicate the need or desire for such programs.

7. He offers special assistance to teachers who are just beginning a program of individualized reading by making materials on philosophy and

methodology available to them as well as by
working especially closely with them during the
early stages of their initiation into the program.

8. He helps teachers to evaluate children's
growth in reading and in the process of communicating these evaluations to parents.

To the question, "When will teachers and librarians work and plan together?" there are at
least three answers. There are the informal contacts that they will normally have in the course
of the school day or week. In some situations
it may be advisable to schedule regular consultation and planning sessions at intervals which
are convenient to both. And, Jo Dewar reports
that her school library is able to lend telling support to the individualized reading program because provision has been made for a faculty-
library committee:

A faculty committee, made up of six teachers from different academic levels functions in an advisory capacity to the librarian
in policy-making and channels requests and recommendations
for books and other library materials to be ordered. They assist
in special projects, such as school-wide Book Week and National
Library Week activities. During the preschool planning period
for teachers each year, they also sponsor an audio-visual training session. . . .[90]

The librarian implements the individualized
reading program through his work with children
by these steps:

1. He helps them locate the right books at the right time. He knows that the principles of seeking and self-selection require a concept of reading guidance which is indirect, subtle, and unobtrusive.

2. He plans for and designs storytelling sessions, periods of reading aloud, and book talks with the understanding that children can most effectively exercise their freedom of self-selection when they have some knowledge of the library's collection in advance and have been stimulated to seek out what they desire.

3. He works with children to develop interesting displays and activities which stimulate their interest in books and which help to motivate the reluctant reader.

4. He plans experiences that will help children to evaluate their reading and channel their reactions to their reading into creative activities.

5. He helps children to become critical readers and thus to constantly improve their reading tastes.

6. He invites individual children or small groups to come to the library during the school day to use its resources to explore personal or curriculum interests.

7. He helps children to solve personal problems and to improve their personal and social

adjustment through books and reading experiences.

8. He invites children to use the library to display their collections, art work, and other creative materials that they have developed as outgrowths of their reading experiences.

The type of schedules that librarians are committed to can help or hinder them in implementing these various aspects of their relationships with children. It appears that the concept of flexibility in library scheduling is gaining favor among educators and librarians. Robert Shadick, a professor at Maryland State Teachers College, commented recently:

> A schedule that keeps the librarian busy giving formal instruction or checking out books prevents the full use of the librarian and the library. The librarian should be available to help a small group do research or to help answer a question raised in classroom discussion. Schedules should be set up that make it possible to accomodate children's interests and enthusiasms which by their nature do not conform to schedules.
> The teacher's willingness to allow children the opportunity to use the library freely will depend largely on her confidence that the pupils will be received in the library. . . .[91]

In schools where the individualized method of reading instruction is used, librarians may be called upon to work with a third group, the parents. Parents may be disturbed when they learn that their children are not having daily lessons with the teacher in a basal reader of a given grade-level of difficulty. Librarians may play an important role here in assisting administrators and teachers to effectively express the meaning and objectives of the program to parents. When the parents understand what the program is, how it works, and where it hopes to go, librarians can offer invaluable assistance in supporting the aims and the objectives in the home setting. Their specialized knowledge of the children's book field ideally equips them to offer advice to interested parents about books they may select for their children's personal libraries. Informal discussions or planned programs, perhaps in cooperation with parent-teacher groups, might encourage families to institute sessions of reading aloud or the sharing and discussions of reading experiences. Librarians can also do much to help parents to appreciate their children's individual interests and needs and to relate these understandings to books and reading.

THE LIBRARIAN AS A TEACHER OF READING

The second hypotheses involved here maintains that in order to make his most effective contribution to the success of the individualized reading program, the elementary school librarian needs to be knowledgeable about the methodology involved in teaching children how to read and in promoting their maximum growth in reading ability and maturity.

I have attempted to point out that the proponents of individualized reading disagree rather fundamentally with the proponents of basal reading instruction, not so much in the enumeration of the basic skills involved in reading but in how these skills are presented to children. The authors of basal reading systems regard the learning of skills as a carefully arranged sequence of teacher-directed lessons that are presented systematically to children step-by-step, much as the principles of arithmetical operations are. If reading could really be taught effectively this way there would be far fewer reading problems in the schools than there presently are, for all the teacher would have to do would be to move page-by-page, sequence-by-sequence through a carefully graduated series of lessons. This is, in fact, the way that modern basal readers and their accompanying manuals are arranged, and basal readers have been for years the foundation of the reading program in the vast majority of elementary schools. Yet the number of nonreaders, poor readers, and reluctant readers in these same schools is legion.

The trouble is, say the proponents of individualized reading instruction, that reading skills cannot be viewed as a series of systematic steps in a teacher's manual or a child's reader or workbook. Reading, they say, must be viewed as part of the behavior exhibited by individual children in their daily lives. Peggy Brogan and Lorene Fox have observed that,

We are gradually coming to realize how individual an affair reading is. When a person reads *he* is the one who seeks. He has the responsibility for bringing his own experience to the author's words—for stretching his own mind as far as it will go in his attempt to find out what the author is saying. Hence individual children will use and require different reading skills at different times, depending upon the unique factors in each of their experiences and ways for learning.[92]

Individualized reading combines the teaching of reading skills with the child's personal experiences in reading; he learns the skills that he needs in reading at the time that he needs to use them and in a setting that he himself has chosen. The belief is that the skills may be taught more economically and learned more effectively and permanently because of the functional setting in which they are presented.

The more that a librarian knows about the skills that are involved in the reading act itself, the more resourceful he can be as he works with teachers and children in individualized reading programs. This, in fact, means that the librarian needs to develop gradually—through experience, consultation with teachers, and professional reading — a better understanding of how language operates in reading. The more comprehension the librarian has of the scope of the reading process, not as a sequence of steps described in a manual but as a recognition of expressed needs on the part of the individualized children and the implications of these needs for required instructional experience, the more confidently and effectively he will be able to assist and guide children in their reading growth. Thus the librarian comes to know the reading skills as an integral continuity growing out of each child's individual experiences, and he introduces increasingly advanced or sophisticated skills as the child's behavior indicates a need for them.

Because of the nature and facilities of the school library, there are certain areas of direct reading instruction that can best be developed by the librarian working cooperatively with the teacher. Florence Cleary, in what has in a short time become a classic work of its kind, developed a comprehensive listing of library-oriented reading skills that are appropriate for most of the children in the middle grades:

I. Locating Information
    1. Learning about all of the resources of the library.
    2. Locating books on library shelves and learning about the general arrangement of libraries.
    3. Understanding the Dewey Classification System.
    4. Learning how to use the card catalog to locate books on the shelves.
    5. Locating and learning the arrangement of picture and pamphlet files and other audio-visual materials in the library.
    6. Learning how to find material in magazines through the use of indexes.

7. Learning how to use library tools and reference books such as encyclopedias and the *World Almanac* to locate desired information.

8. Learning how to use all parts of a book to locate information—the index, graphs, maps, charts, appendix, and illustrations.

II. Selecting and Organizing Information

1. Help pupils understand what the author is saying.

2. Teach them to look up the meaning of words in the dictionary.

3. Help pupils choose information that has particular use and meaning in relation to the purpose they have for reading.

4. Help pupils select the most important ideas and facts and arrange them in some kind of logical order.

5. Help them arrange less important facts under main headings, either in the form of notes or in the outline form.

III. Analyzing and Interpreting Information.

By adroit questioning and guidance, help children to:

1. Select and organize all facts related to a pertinent problem.

2. Understand all the ideas and concepts presented.

3. Consider all the possible relationships in the information i.e., time, place, cause, effect.

4. React to the information.

IV. Reaching Conclusions and Utilizing Information and Knowledge

In the middle grades the inventive teacher constantly helps the children to interpret information and reach conclusions to the end that they may refine their opinions and form judgments . . . he promotes the habit of reflection.[93]

Librarians, like teachers, need to learn as much as they can about the nature and method of the reading process. Many questions about how children learn to read and how the techniques that they employ in reading may change as they mature remain unanswered. Some recent studies, such as those by William Gray and Bernice Rogers[94] and Mary Austin and her associates,[95] have raised more questions than they have answered about reading practices in the schools. Proponents of individualized reading, however, believe that the whole question of reading methodology and skills must never obscure the importance of a way of thinking about reading instruction which, "has its basis in ego-enchantment and builds upon the premise that as the individual develops good feelings toward himself, he becomes free to accomplish his best thinking and his deepest learning.[96]

INDIVIDUALIZED READING'S IMPACT
ON THE LIBRARY

Those writers who pioneered in the development of individualized reading as an educationally sound and workable program of instruction recognized from the beginning the important role that the library and the librarian would play in implementing their principles and objectives. Even as they encouraged teachers working in schools that were deprived of the services of a trained librarian, and indeed in many cases even of a centralized library collection, to experiment with the method that they advocated, they insisted on the advisability of staffing elementary schools with trained librarians. Helen Mackintosh, Chief of the Elementary School Section of the U.S. Office of Education, and Mary Mahar, Children's Library Specialist in the same bureau, have commented on the need for elementary school librarians to service the program:

Teaching reading by the individualized method requires plentiful resources of children's books. An elementary school library with an organized collection of children's books and other material, administered by a professional librarian and open at all times of the school day to teachers and children, is essential to a fully developed reading program in the elementary school. From it, with the assistance of the librarian, teachers can select classroom collections which they can continually refresh by making new selections. . .

In the reading program designed to serve . . . highly individual needs, the elementary school library not only provides a valuable service, but provides it economically.[97]

Beyond the immediate aims of teaching children how to read and promoting their reading skills and abilities to the highest potential for each child, the ultimate objective of individualized reading as a method of instruction in the elementary school is to produce the kind of individuals who will have an on-going love of reading, mature readers who have come to appreciate the many benefits and pleasures that books and reading have to offer. To the librarian, the program of individualized instruction in reading means that he will be taking a more active part in the reading program—the core of the elementary school's curriculum—than he has had an opportunity to take in the past. It means that his services and the facilities and resources of the library will become indispensable to the operation of the school. Should individualized reading practices become more widespread, as they show every promise of doing, it means that the schools will be producing a citizenry far more acutely aware of the enormous advantages that books and libraries have to offer, a citizenry much more likely to patronize the library after they have completed their years of schooling, and thus more sympathetic to the need for supporting the library and its services.

Noting that in some situations, when schools without a staff librarian have launched into an individualized reading program, it has been necessary to call in the public librarian for advice and assistance, Patrick Groff gazes into a somewhat chaotic but tantalizing future:

Because individualized reading is not as yet widespread enough, the call on public librarians to visit schools to explain the collection can usually be met. Imagine, however if three or four schools without librarians suddenly decide to individualize their reading programs. If they were served by a single public library, how long would it take before the librarian would run out of books, time, and energy? Handled properly, the situation would bring to the attention of citizens reluctant to pay enough for their schools, the need to spend more money for the books their children read in schools.

As the status of books in the minds of the general public grows, so grows the status of the librarian. It is axiomatic that the person who reads little or the person who reads material of a decidedly low literary value, sees little need for the improvement of library service or the betterment of librarian's salaries or working conditions. . . There should be long-range benefits not only for society in general, but for the librarians as well, from the use of individualized reading.[98]

SOME UNSOLVED PROBLEMS

There are indications that individualized reading instruction is becoming more widespread in elementary schools. The recent publication of enthusiastic comment and highly encouraging research results by the school system of New York City has interested an increasing number of school administrators and educators in surrounding counties. Several systems in Nassau and Suffolk Counties are now experimenting with individualized reading, especially in the fourth, fifth, and sixth grades, when most children have become fairly independent readers.[99]

If the movement takes substantial hold it will undoubtedly have a telling effect on the demand for professionally trained librarians and for greatly expanded library facilities at the elementary school level. Such a trend would have enormous advantages for the library profession, but it would also suggest a number of problems that need further attention. Among these are:

1. Measured in terms of their ability to choose books of appropriate difficulty and purpose, how effective are children of various ages, grades, and reading levels in the process of the self-selection of their reading materials?

2. Is there a best time to initiate individualized reading instruction? Some authorities claim that individualized reading may be used effectively at the first-grade level, others feel that it may be best to postpone its use until the third or fourth grade.

3. What patterns of scheduling seem to be best suited to the facilitation of library services in schools which have adopted the individualized method of instruction either in reading or in other areas of the curriculum as well?

4. What are the most effective ways of keeping teachers informed about the library and its resources, particularly in respect to the content of the individualized titles that constitute the collection and the appropriate use of certain books for specific educational aims?

5. How do individualized reading programs materially affect policies of book selection in the library? To what extent will the implementation of such programs affect budget allotments and staff requirements in the library?

6. Is it possible to more precisely define—theoretically and operationally—exactly how reading guidance can be effectively directive without violating the principles of seeking and self-selection?

The fundamental problem now facing many educators involves the question of whether there really are two opposing approaches to reading instruction, or whether, as Paul Witty[100] has suggested, the best features of basal reading may be combined with the best features of individualized reading. In her reply to Dr. Witty, Jeanette Veatch stated that there are indeed two opposing systems, "and the two are irreconcilable.".[101] She suggests what is, perhaps, the most urgent question of all: To what extent does the current conventional ability-grouping affect the mental health of our nation's children?

APPENDIX

CITATIONS

1. Mortimer Adler, *How to Read a Book,* (New York, Simon and Schuster, 1955), p. 63.

2. Mark Sullivan, *Our Times: The United States, 1900-1925,* (New York, Scribners, 1927), II, 15.

3. Paul Witty, *Reading in Modern Education* (Boston, Heath, 1949), pp. 5-6.

4. William Gray, *On Their Own in Reading* (Chicago, Scott, Foresman, 1948), pp. 26-27.

5. Walter Barbe, *Educator's Guide to Personalized Reading Instruction* (Englewood Cliffs, N. J., Prentice-Hall, 1961), p. 9.

6. Allan McMahan, "Make Friends with Your Bookseller," *The Wonderful World of Books* (New York, New American Library, 1952), p. 226.

7. Paul Witty, "Individualized Reading—a Summary and Evaluation," *Elementary English,* 36:401-12, October, 1959.

8. Jeannette Veatch, *Individualizing Your Reading Program* (New York, Putnam, 1959), p. xii.

9. Constance McCullough, "Opinions Differ on Individualized Reading," *N.E.A. Journal,* 47:163, March, 1958.

10. J. Veatch, *Individualizing Your Reading Program,* pp. vii-viii.

11. American Association of School Librarians, *Standards for School Library Programs* (Chicago, American Library Association, 1960), p. 15.

12. Jean Lowrie, "Elementary School Libraries Today," *New Definitions of School Library Service* (Chicago, University of Chicago, 1960), p.29.

13. Mary Gaver, "Research on Elementary School Libraries," *A.L.A.Bulletin,* 56:123. February, 1962.

14. Russell Stauffer, "Individualized Reading Instruction—a Backward Look," *Elementary English,* 36:335-41, May, 1959.

15. Paul Witty, "Individualized Reading—a Summary and Evaluation," p. 401.

16. William Gray, "Role of Group and Individualized Teaching in a Sound Reading Program," *The Reading Teacher*, 11:99-104, December, 1957.

17. Helen Darrow and Virgil Howes, *Approaches to Individualized Reading* (New York, Appleton-Century-Crofts, 1960) pp. 1-5.

18. Alvina Burrows, *Teaching Children in the Middle Grades* Boston, Heath, 1952), pp. 166, 174.

19. Veatch, *Individualizing Your Reading Program*.

20. *Ibid.*, pp. 3-4.

21. *Ibid.*, pp. 14-18.

22. A. E. Traxler, *Eight More Years of Research in Reading* (New York, Educational Records Bureau, 1955), p. 4.

23. William Sheldon, *Influences Upon Reading Instruction in the United States* (Syracuse, N. Y., Syracuse University Press 1961), p. 12.

24. Willard Olson, "Seeking, Self-Selection, and Pacing in the Use of Books by Children," *The Packet* (Boston, Heath, Spring, 1952), pp. 3-10.

25. *Ibid.*, pp. 3-4.

26. *Ibid.*, p. 6.

27. May Lazar, in a speech delivered at the 1957 Conference of the International Reading Association, New York City, and reprinted in Veatch, *Individualizing Your Reading Program*, pp. 192-202.

28. *Ibid.*, pp. 194-95.

29. Jeannette Veatch, "Individualized Reading—for Success in the Classroom," *The Educational Trend*, No. 654 (New London, Conn., Arthur Croft, 1954) p. 2.

30. Veatch, *Individualizing Your Reading Program*, p. x.

31. Peggy Brogan and Lorene Fox, *Helping Children Read* (New York, Holt, Rinehart, and Winston, 1961), pp. 86-88.

32. Jeannette Veatch, "Children's Interests and Individualized Reading," *The Reading Teacher*, 10:160-65, February, 1957).

33. Harlan Shores and Herbert Rudman, *What Children Are Interested In* (Chicago, Spencer Press, 1954).

34. George Norvell, *What Boys and Girls Like to Read* (Morristown, N. J., Silver Burdett, 1958).

35. Darrow and Howes, p. 32.

36. Nancy Larrick, *A Teacher's Guide to Children's Books* (Columbus, Ohio, Merrill, 1960), pp. 85-86.

37. Donald Durrell, *Improving Reading Instruction* (New York, World, 1956), pp. 143-44.

38. Virgil Howes, "Guidance Through Books, *School Libraries*, 9:9-11, May 1959,.

39. *Ibid.*, p. 10-11.

40. Barbe, *Educator's Guide to Personalized Reading Instruction*, pp. 70-74.

41. Olson, p. 8.

42. Paul Hazard, *Books, Children and Men*, (Horn Book, 1944), p. 49.

43. Norvell, p. 282.

44. William Burton, Clara Baker, and Grace Kemp, *Reading in Child Development* (New York, Bobbs-Merrill, 1956), pp. 367-68.

45. May Arbuthnot, *Children and Books* (Chicago, Scott, Foresman, 1957), p. 16.

46. *Ibid.*, pp. 545-48.

47. Nancy Larrick, "You Need Good Libraries to Teach Reading Today," *Junior Libraries*, 2:29, September 15, 1954.

48. Norvell, pp. 182-86.

49. Mary Ann Daniel, "You Can Individualize Your Reading Program, Too," *Elementary English*, 33:444-446, November, 1956.

50. *Ibid.*, p. 446.

51. Phyllis Parkin, "An Individualized Program of Reading," *Educational Leadership*, 14:34-38, October, 1956.

52. *Ibid.*, p. 38.

53. Burrows, *Teaching Children in the Middle Grades*, pp. 170-71.

54. *Ibid.*, p. 172.

55. Darrow and Howes, pp. 43-44.

56. Brogan and Fox, pp. 36-39.

57. Jo Dewar, "An Individualized Reading Program in an Elementary School Library," *A.L.A. Bulletin*, 56:114-15, February, 1962.

58. Jean Lowrie, *Elementary School Libraries*; (New York, Scarecrow Press, 1961), p. 135.

59. Dewar, p. 116.

60. Veatch, *Individualizing Your Reading Program*. p. 52.

61. *Ibid.*, p. 53.

62. Barbe, *Educator's Guide to Personalized Reading Instruction*, pp. 47-48.

63. Veatch, *Individualizing Your Reading Program*, p. 23.

64. Barbe, *Educator's Guide to Personalized Reading Instruction*, pp. 131-207.

65. *Ibid.*, pp. 192-93.

66. Adapted from an unpublished list of suggestions for grouping developed by Alvina Burrows for use with her teacher-training classes at School of Education, New York University.

67. Paul McKee, *An Instructional Program for the Fourth, Fifth, and Sixth Grades* (Boston, Houghton Mifflin, 1957),pp. 6-7.

68. Lillian Gray and Dora Reese, *Teaching Children to Read* (New York, Ronald Press, 1957), pp. 241-42.

69. Larrick, *A Teacher's Guide to Children's Books*, p. 148.

70. Burrows, *Teaching Children in the Middle Grades*, p. 173.

71. Association for Childhood Education, *Literature with Children* (Washington, D. C., Association for Childhood Education, 1961), p. 25.

72. Maida Sharpe, "Individualized Reading: Follow-up Activities," *Elementary English*,36:21-23, January, 1959.

73. Gray, *On Their Own in Reading*, pp. 106-22, 228-57.

74. Florence Cleary, *Blueprints for Better Reading* (New York, H. W. Wilson, 1957), pp. 182-203.

75. Association for Childhood Education, pp. 19-23.

76. Ann Noel, "Twelve-Year-Old Dave Learns to Read," *Individualizing Reading Practices* (New York, Bureau of Publications, Teachers College, Columbia University, 1958), pp. 81-84.

77. *Ibid.*, p. 81.

78. *Ibid.*, p. 84.

79. Burrows, *Teaching Children in the Middle Grades*, pp. 199-200.

80. Mary Largent,"My Third-Graders Are Eager Readers," *N.E.A. Journal*, 48:64-65, March, 1959.

81. Parkin, pp. 37-38.

82. Clare Walker, *An Evaluation of Two Programs of Reading In Grades Four, Five, and Six*, doctoral dissertation (New York, School of Education, New York University, 1957).

83. Robert Karlin, "Some Reactions to Individualized Reading," *The Reading Teacher*, 11:95-98, December, 1957.

84. Irene Vite, "Individualized Reading—the Scoreboard on Control Studies," *Education*, 81:285-90, January, 1961.

85. Harold Karr, "An Experiment with an Individualized Method of Teaching Reading," *The Reading Teacher*, 7:174-77, February, 1954.

86. Miriam Aronow, "A Study of the Effect of Individualized Reading on Children's Reading Test Scores,"*The Reading Teacher*, 15:86-91, November, 1961.

87. Described in *A Practical Guide to Individualized Reading*, Publication No. 40, (New York, Bureau of Educational Research, Board of Education, New York City, 1960).

88. Aronow, p. 91.

89. Beatrice Hurley, *"Curriculum for Elementary School Children,"* (New York, Ronald Press, 1957), pp. 218-19.

90. Dewar, p. 117.

91. Robert Shadick, "The Schoool Librarian: Key to Curriculum Development, "*Elementary School Journal*, 62:301-302 March, 1962.

92. Brogan and Fox, p. 92.

93. Cleary, *Blueprints for Better Reading*, pp. 160-72.

94. William Gray and Bernice Rogers, *Maturity in Reading* (Chicago, University of Chicago Press, 1956), p. 273.

95. Mary Austin, et al., *The Torch Lighters: Tomorrow's Teachers of Reading* (Cambridge, Mass., Harvard University Press, 1961), p. 191.

96. Darrow and Howes, p. 28.

97. Helen Mackintosh and Mary Mahar, "Teaching Reading the Individualized Way," *School Life*, 40:4-7, May, 1958.

98. Patrick Groff, "The Librarian and Individualized Reading," *Wilson Library Bulletin*, 34:360-61, January, 1960.

99. According to informed comment by several teachers and administrators at the Suffolk Zone Teachers' Conference, held in October, 1962.

100. Witty, "Individualized Reading—a Summary and Evaluation," p. 412.

101. Jeannette Veatch, "In Defense of Individualized Reading," *Elementary English*, 37:227-34, April, 1960.

BIBLIOGRAPHY

Acinapuro, Philip, *A Comparative Study of the Results of Two Reading Programs—An Individualized Pattern and a Three Ability Group Pattern*, Doctoral dissertation, New York, Teachers College, Columbia University, 1959.

Anderson, Irving, Byron Hughes, and Robert Dixon, "The Relationship between Reading Achievement and the Method of Teaching Reading," *University of Michigan School of Education Bulletin*, 5:104-8, April, 1956.

Arbuthnot, May, *Children and Books*, 2d ed.,Chicago, Scott Foresman, 1957.

Aronow, Miriam, "A Study of the Effect of Individualized Reading on Children's Reading Test Scores," *The Reading Teacher*, 15:86-91, November, 1961.

Association for Childhood Education, *Literature with Children*, Washington, D. C., Association for Childhood Education International, 1961.

Austin, Mary, et al., *The Torch Lighters: Tomorrow's Teachers of Reading*, Cambridge, Mass., Harvard University Press, 1961.

Barbe, Walter, *Educator's Guide to Personalized Reading Instruction*, Englewood Cliffs, N. J., Prentice-Hall, 1961.

——"Personalized or Individualized Reading Instruction, *Education*, 81:537-40, May, 1961.

Blake, H. E. "Here's Another Way," in the portfolio, *Creative Ways in Teaching the Language Arts*, Champaign, Ill., National Council of Teachers of English, 1957.

Bohnhorst, Ben and Sophia Sellars, "Individualized Reading Instruction *vs.* Basal Textbook Instruction: Some Tentative Explorations, *"Elementary English*, 36:185-90, March, 1959.

Bonny, Jill and Levin Hanigan, "Individualized Teaching of Reading," *34th Yearbook of the National Elementary School Principal*, Washington, D. C., Association of Elementary School Principals, 1955.

Brogan, Peggy and Lorene Fox, *Helping Children Read*, New York, Holt, Rinehart and Winston, 1961.

Bureau of Educational Research, Board of Education, City of New York, *A Practical Guide to Individualized Reading*, New York, Bureau of Publications, B. of Ed., City of New York, 1960.

Burrows, Alvina, "Caste System or Democracy?" *Elementary English*, 27:145-47, March, 1950.

——*Teaching Children in the Middle Grades*, Boston, D. C. Heath, 1952.

Burton, William, Clara Baker, and Grace Kemp, *Reading in Child Development*, New York, Bobbs-Merrill, 1956.

Cadenhead, Kenneth, "Plan for Individualized Reading Instruction," *Elementary English*, 39:260-62, March, 1962.

California State Department of Education, "Reading Instruction through Self-Selection, "*California Journal of Elementary Education*, 27:135-87, February, 1959.

Carr, Constance, *Individualized Development of Abilities and Skills in Reading*, Doctoral dissertation, New York, Teachers College, Columbia University, 1958.

Carson, Louise, "Moving Toward Individualization," *Elementary English*, 34:362-66, October, 1957.

Cavanaugh, C. L."Every Child's Reading Needs Are Unique," *Instructor*, 68:19, 106, March, 1959.

Cleary, Florence, *Blueprints for Better Reading*, New York, H. W. Wilson, 1957.

——"School Library and the Changing Curriculum," *Educational Leadership*, 16:176-81, December, 1958.

Crossley, Ruth, "An Individualized Reading Program, " *Elementary English*, 36:16-20, January, 1959.

Daniel,Mary Ann, "You Can Individualize Your Reading Program, Too,"*Elementary English*, 33:444-46, November,1956.

Darrow, Helen and Virgil Howes, *Approaches to Individualized Reading*, New York, Appleton-Century-Crofts, 1960.

Dewar, Jo, "An Individualized Reading Program in an Elementary School Library," *A.L.A. Bulletin*, 56:113-16, February, 1962.

Dickhart, Audrey, "Breaking the Lock-Step in Reading," *Elementary English*, 35:54-56, January, 1958

Dolch, Edward, "Groups in Reading," *Elementary English* 31:477-84, December, 1954.

——"What Next in the Teaching of Reading?" *Education* 78:526-28, May, 1958.

Ducker, Sam, "Research Report: Effects of Introducing an Individualized Reading Approach by Student Teachers," *Reading in Action*, New York, Scholastic Magazines, 1957.

Durrell, Donald, *Improving Reading Instruction*, New York, World, 1956.

Evans, Dean, "Individualized Reading Program," *Elementary English*, 30:275-80, May, 1953.

——"Individualized Reading Program for the Elementary School," *Elementary School Journal*, 54:157-62, November, 1953.

Fay, Leo, "Trends in Teaching of Elementary Reading," *Phi Delta Kappan*, 41:345-48, May, 1960.

Floyd, Cecil, "Meeting Children's Reading Needs in the Middle Grades of the Elementary School," *Elementary School Journal*, 55:99-101, October, 1959.

Garretson, Grace, "How One School Read the Needs of the Slow Reader," *19th Yearbook of the Claremont College Reading Conference*, Claremont, Calif., Claremont College, 1954.

Gates, Arthur, "The Future of Research in Reading," *Education*, 82:545-54, May, 1962.

——"Unsolved Problems in Reading," *Elementary English* 31:331-34, October, 1954.

Gaver, Mary, "Research on Elementary School Libraries," *A.L.A. Bulletin*, 52:119-24, February, 1962.

Gordon, Ira, and Christine Clark, "An Experiment in Individualized Reading," *Childhood Education*, 38:112-13, November, 1961.

Gray, Lillian and Dora Reese, *Teaching Children to Read*, New York, Ronald Press, 1957.

Gray, William, *On Their Own in Reading*, 2d ed. Chicago, Scott, Foresman, 1960.

——"Role of Group and Individualized Teaching in a Sound Reading Program," *The Reading Teacher*, 11:99-104, December, 1957.

Gray, William, and Bernice Rogers, *Maturity in Reading*, Chicago, University of Chicago Press, 1956.

Greenman, Ruth, "Individualized Reading in Third and Fourth Grades," *Elementary English*, 36:234-37, April, 1959.

Groff, Patrick, "Getting Started with Individualized Reading," *Elementary English*, 37:105-12, February, 1960.

——"Librarian and Individualized Reading," *Wilson Library Bulletin*, 31:449-50, February, 1957.

——"Material for Individualized Reading," *Elementary English*, 38;1-7, January, 1957.

Guinzburg, Harold, "Educate Students So They Want to Read," *Wilson Library Bulletin*, 31:449-50, February, 1957.

Gurney, Tess, "My Individualized Reading Program," *Childhood Education*, 32:334-36, March, 1956.

Hanna, Geneva, and Mariana McAllister, *Books, Young People, and Reading Guidance*, New York, Harper, 1960.

Hildreth, Gertrude, *Teaching Reading*, New York, Holt, 1958.

——"Individualized Reading Instruction," *Teachers College Record*, 42:123-37, November, 1950.

Howes, Virgil, "Guidance through Reading," *School Libraries*, 9:9-11, May, 1959.

Hurley, Beatrice, *Curriculum for Elementary School Children*, New York, Ronald Press, 1957.

Jacobs, Leland, "Reading on Their Own Means Reading at Their Growing Edges," *The Reading Teacher*, 6:27-36, March, 1953.

Jenkins, Marian, "Here's to Success in Reading—Self-Selection Helps," *Childhood Education*, 32:124-31, November, 1955.

——"Self-Selection in Reading", *The Reading Teacher*, 11:84-90, December, 1957.

Johnson, Eleanor, *Individualizing Reading*, Curriculum Letter No. 35, Middletown, Conn., Wesleyan University, 1957.

Karlin, Robert, "Some Reactions to Individualized Reading," *The Reading Teacher*, 11:95-98, December, 1957.

Karr, Harold, "An Experiment with an Individualized Method of Teaching Reading," *The Reading Teacher*, 7:174-77, February, 1954.

Kessie, Eleanor, "Good-by to Reading in Groups," *Grade Teacher*, 78:30, November, 1960.

Kingsley, Marjorie, "An Experiment in Individualized Reading," *Elementary English*, 35:113-18, February, 1958.

Largent, Mary, "My Third Graders Are Eager Readers" *N.E.A. Journal*, 48:64-65, March, 1959.

Larrick, Nancy, *A Parent's Guide to Children's Reading*, Garden City, N.Y., Doubleday, 1958.

———*A Teacher's Guide to Children's Books*, Columbus, Ohio, Charles Merrill, 1960.

———"You Need Good Libraries to Teach Reading Today," *Junior Libraries*, 2:25-31, September 15, 1954.

Lazar, May, "Individualized Reading—A Dynamic Approach," *The Reading Teacher*, 11:75-83, December, 1957.

Lee, J. Murray, "Individualized Instruction," *Education*, 74: 279-83, January, 1954.

Lowrie, Jean, "Elementary School Libraries Today," *New Definitions of School Library Service*, Chicago, University of Chicago Press, 1960.

MacBean, Dilla, "Modern Reading Program and the School Library," *A.L.A. Bulletin*, 51:81-82, February, 1957.

McCullough, Constance, "Opinions Differ on Individualized Reading," *N.E.A. Journal*, 47:163-166, March, 1958.

———"What Does Research Reveal About Practices in Reading," *English Journal*, 46:475-90, November, 1957.

McKee, Paul, "*An Instructional Program for the Fourth, Fifth, and Sixth Grades*, Boston, Houghton Mifflin, 1957,.

Mackintosh, Helen, and Mary Mahar, "Teaching Reading the Individualized Way," *School Life*, 40:4-7, May, 1958.

McVey, Marcia, "Reading Sure Is Fun Now," *Elementary English*, 37:307-9, May, 1960.

Maib, Frances, Individualized Reading, *Elementary English*, 29:84-89, February, 1952.

Maxey, Bessie, "Individualized Reading Program," *Instructor*, 62:47, 78, January, 1953.

Miel, Alice, ed. *Individualizing Reading Practices*, New York, Bureau of Publications, Teachers College, Columbia University, 1958.

National Council of Teachers of English, *Language Arts for Today's Children*, New York, Appleton-Century-Crofts, 1954.

Norvell, George, *What Boys and Girls Like to Read*, Morristown, N.J., Silver Burdett, 1958.

Olson, Willard, "Seeking, Self-Selection, and Pacing in the Use of Books," *The Packet*, Boston, D.C.Heath, Spring, 1952.

Orr, Evelyn, "Personalized Reading," *Elementary English*, 38:227-28, April, 1961.

Parkin, Phyllis, "An Individualized Program of Reading," *Educational Leadership*, 14:34-38, October, 1956.

Picozzi, Adelaide, "An Approach to Individualized Reading," *Elementary English*, 35:302-4, May, 1958.

Pozner, A. N. "Individualized Reading," *Education*, 82:183-86, November, 1961.

Robinson, Helen, "Individualized Reading," *Elementary School Journal*, 60:411-26, May, 1960.

Rothrock,Dayton,"Heterogenous, Homogenous, or Individualized Approach to Reading," *Elementary English*, 38:233-35, April, 1961.

Rowe, Ruth, and Ester Dornhoefer, "Individualized Reading: as a Principal Sees It; as a Teacher Sees It, "*Childhood Education*, 34:118-22, November, 1957.

Safford, Alton, "Evaluation of an Individualized Reading Program," *The Reading Teacher*, 13:266-70, April, 1960.

Sartain, Harry, "Research on Individualized Reading," *Education*, 81:515-20, May, 1961.

——"The Roseville Experiment with Individualized Reading," *The Reading Teacher*, 13:227-31, April, 1960.

Shadick, Robert, "The School Librarian: Key to Curriculum Development," *Elementary School Journal*, 62:298-303, March, 1962.

Sharpe, Maida, "Individualized Reading: Follow-up Activities," *Elementary English*, 36:21-24, January, 1959.

——"Individualized Reading Program," *Elementary English*, 35:507:12, December, 1958.

Sheldon, William, *Influences Upon Reading Instruction in the United States*, Syracuse, N. Y., Syracuse University Press, 1961.

Stauffer, Russell, "Individualized and Group Type Directed Reading Instruction," *Elementary English*, 37:375-82, October, 1960.

——"Individualizing Reading Instruction: a Backward Look," *Elementary English*, 36:335-41, March, 1959.

Strickland, Ruth, "Making the Most of Children's Interests in the Teaching of Reading," *The Reading Teacher*, 10:137-38, February, 1957.

Stuart, Allaire, "Individualized Reading," *Elementary English*, 39:256-59, March, 1962.

Thompson, Mildred, "Why Not Try Self-Selection?" *Elementary English*, 33:486-90, December, 1956.

Tooze, Ruth, *Your Children Want to Read*, Englewood Cliffs, N.J., Prentice-Hall, 1957.

Veatch, Jeanette, "Children's Interests and Individualized Reading," *The Reading Teacher*, 10:160-65, February, 1957.

——"In Defense of Individualized Reading," *Elementary English*, 37:227-34, April, 1960.

——*Individualizing Your Reading Program*, New York, Putnam's, 1959.

Vite, Irene, "Grouping Practices in Individualized Reading," *Elementary English*, 38:91-98, February, 1961.

——"Individualized Reading: the Scoreboard on Control Studies," *Education*, 81:285-90.

Walker, Clare, *An Evaluation of Two Programs in Reading in Grades Four, Five, and Six of the Elementary School*, Doctoral dissertation, New York, School of Education, New York University, 1957.

Wilson, Harriet, "Stop Reading in Ability Groups," *Instructor* 65:35,74, April, 1956.

Wilt, Miriam, "Another way to Meet Individual Differences," *Elementary English*, 35:26-28, January, 1958.

Witty, Paul, "Individualized Reading—a Summary and Evaluation," *Elementary English*, 36:401-12, October, 1959.

——"Reading Instruction . . . a Forward Look," *Elementary English*, 38:151-64, March, 1961.

Young, Marion, "A Report on Self-Selection in Reading," *Elementary English*, 35:176-81, March, 1958.

INDEX